The Good City

A Study of Urban Development and
Policy in Britain

D1621189

The Good City

A Study of Urban Development and
Policy in Britain

David Donnison with **Paul Soto**

HEINEMANN

Heinemann Educational Books Ltd
22 Bedford Square, London WC1B 3HH

LONDON EDINBURGH MELBOURNE AUCKLAND
HONG KONG SINGAPORE KUALA LUMPUR NEW DELHI
IBADAN NAIROBI JOHANNESBURG
EXETER (NH) KINGSTON PORT OF SPAIN

British Library Cataloguing in Publication Data

Donnison, David Vernon
    The good city. — (Centre for Environmental
Studies. Series).
    1. Cities and towns — Great Britain
    I. Title   II. Soto, Paul   III. Series
    309.2'62'0941   HT133

    ISBN 0-435-85216-7
    ISBN 0-435-85217-5 Pbk

Typeset by The Castlefield Press of High Wycombe
in 10/12pt Journal Roman, and printed in Great Britain
by Richard Clay (The Chaucer Press) Ltd, Bungay, Suffolk

Contents

Preface

David Donnison started work on this study at the Centre for Environmental Studies in 1973, publishing his first ideas and intentions in *New Society* a few weeks later.[1] Paul Soto joined him the following year and he was responsible for the empirical work in Chapters 5 to 9 and for writing the first drafts of these chapters. Donnison was responsible for formulating the central questions to be studied, the social and political ideas brought to bear upon them, and the final drafts of all chapters.

We thank the Social Science Research Council for funding this study, and the Centre for Environmental Studies and later − on a part-time basis − the Policy Studies Institute for enabling us to work on it.

We are particularly grateful to Richard Webber, then at CES, for the help he gave us with the cluster analysis used in Part II. We collaborated closely with Hilary Robinson, Peter Wedge and Peter Gorbach at the National Children's Bureau. They commented helpfully on many of our chapters, and without their help Chapter 11 could not have been written. Phillip Jackman helped in the early stages of the study. We gained much useful advice from Gordon Cameron, Alex Catalano, Doreen Massey and Ray Pahl. Kay Carmichael gave encouragement at a crucial stage. Gerald Smart was our patient and supportive link with the SSRC.

We thank Edwin Brown, Sir Alec Clegg, Barry Cullingworth, Madeline Drake, Alan Evans, David Gleave, Graham Gudgin, Barbara Kahan, Maurice Kogan, Alice Perkins, Maurice Speed and Nancy Westlake, all of whom commented on one or more chapters.

Irene Morrish worked with us throughout the study, searching for references, administering the survey reported in Chapter 12 and patiently and accurately typing what must have seemed endless drafts of this book. We are enormously grateful to her.

Since we worked at the Centre for Environmental Studies, Donnison has moved to the Supplementary Benefits Commission and Soto to the North Kensington Law Centre, but neither of these organisations is in any way responsible for our findings or the conclusions we draw from them.

David Donnison
Paul Soto
October 1979

List of Tables, Figures and Maps

Part I

ONUS → Distribution of industry act
regulate & choose industry 1945

new New Towns act 1946
permit buildings bar

National parks + access to countryside
acts
1949
Town development act 1952.

1 Town Planning in Britain: the Coalition of 1947

The Coalition of 1947

The history of British town and country planning is the story of the rise and fall of a loosely knit alliance — the creation over several generations of a reforming coalition of diverse groups with common interests in the orderly management of land, and the recent disintegration of that coalition. There is no need to tell the first part of the story for it has been told many times before,[1] and it is too early to tell the second with detachment; we are still living through it.[2] But the evolution of British ideas about planning must be briefly recalled at the start of this book because that story is the context of our study and the questions we shall be asking.

Lewis Silkin summoned a coalition representing various interests to his support when he introduced the Bill which became the Town and Country Planning Act of 1947. This law gave Counties and County Boroughs a duty to regulate nearly all development of land, interpreting 'development' in a very comprehensive manner to include changes in the use of land and buildings, the erection of new buildings, the extension of old ones, changes in their external appearance, and outdoor advertising. The new planning authorities were required to prepare and publish development plans for their areas and to revise them regularly. The Act was also designed to acquire for the state all increases in land values brought about by development. Its provisions created the profession which administers these powers.

The Town and Country Planning Act was the most important in a series of five Acts, passed within seven years, which together created a planning system that has not been fundamentally changed since. The others were the Distribution of Industry Act 1945 giving powers to regulate the location of industry and to attract industrialists to chosen regions; the New Towns Act 1946 providing for the building of new towns by public development corporations; the National Parks and Access to the Countryside Act 1949 giving planning authorities powers to run countryside parks with advice from a central commission; and the Town Development Act 1952 enabling big cities, with help from the central government, to collaborate with smaller towns which are prepared to take some of their people.

Silkin was well aware that he was introducing a historic measure in January 1947. His two hour speech began with an exposition of 'the objects of town and country planning'. These, he said,

are becoming increasingly understood and accepted. Primarily, they are to secure a proper balance between the competing demands for land, so that all the land of the country is used in the best interests of the whole people. . . . [Land would be needed for] the housing programme, including the clearance of slums and the rebuilding of blitzed areas, the redevelopment of obsolete and badly laid out areas, the dispersal of population and industry from our large, overcrowded cities to new towns . . . the expansion of the social services, particularly the new schools . . . the construction of new and wider roads . . . and the needs of the Service Departments for land for training and experimental purposes.

On the other hand, town and country planning must preserve land from development. A high level of agricultural production is vital. More land must be kept for forestry. We have to see that our mineral resources . . . are properly developed and are not unnecessarily sterilised by erecting buildings on the surface. And it is important to safeguard the beauty of the countryside and coast-line [in order to] enable more people to enjoy them, and because we must develop the tourist industry as a source of foreign exchange.

. . . these conflicting demands for land must be dovetailed together. If each is considered in isolation, the common interest is bound to suffer. Housing must be so located in relation to industry that workers are not compelled to make long, tiring and expensive journeys to and from work. Nor must our already large towns be permitted to sprawl, and expand, so as to eat up the adjacent rural areas and make access to the countryside and to the amenities in the centre of the town more difficult. Green belts must be left round towns, and the most fertile land must be kept for food production. The continued drift from the countryside must be arrested. . . . between the wars, industry tended to concentrate in the South of England, with the result that towns in the South, especially London, grew too large for health, efficiency and safety, while some of the older industrial areas suffered chronic unemployment.[3]

Henceforth such 'social evils' must be 'corrected'. Silkin was, in effect, reading Parliament a roll-call of the interests which had assembled round the cause of town planning: the public health movement founded by Chadwick and the great medical officers of the previous century; the philanthropic and municipal housing movements, and the campaigners for new towns; farmers, country gentlemen and commuters who wanted to conserve agricultural land and the beauties of rural England, the authorities responsible for roads, public transport and water supplies, and the mining and quarrying industries; the Labour movement and the hunger marchers from Jarrow and Clydeside; the educationists, the tourist trade; and even the Ministry of Defence. All, he argued, had an interest in the Act and would benefit from the work of the profession it was to create. Silkin's appeal was well-judged. Although the Opposition felt obliged to vote against the measure for what they felt to be its technical failings, no speaker questioned its fundamental purposes.

Planners were not simply to be technicians who would content themselves with the orderly management of competing demands for land: they were a movement, expected to play their part in creating a new world. Eight months before, when introducing the New Towns Bill, Silkin had reminded Parliament of the movement's history, leading the House from Sir Thomas More's *Utopia* and Queen Elizabeth I's unsuccessful attempt to restrain the growth of London, via the early utopian communities and Ebenezer Howard's vision of new towns to the great wartime Reports on the distribution of the industrial population[4] and the redevelopment of London.[5] The new towns which the government planned to create were to be very different communities from the middle-class suburbs and working-class council estates built between the wars. In Silkin's words:

The new towns must provide accommodation for people of all income limits. We must not make them towns inhabited by people of one income level, and that the lowest. . . . The primary schools will be so situated that no child need travel more than a quarter of a mile to school. A much higher proportion of the land in the new town can be made available for public open spaces and playing fields, close to the homes instead of many miles away. . . . The towns will be divided into neighbourhood units, each unit with its own shops, schools, open spaces, community halls and other amenities. . . . I am most anxious that the planning should be such that the different income groups living in the new towns will not be segregated. . . . I want to see the new towns gay and bright, with plenty of theatres, concert halls, and meeting places. . . . They must be so laid out that there is ready access to the countryside for all.

He concluded on a high note: 'we may well produce in the new towns a new type of citizen, a healthy, self-respecting, dignified person with a sense of beauty, culture and civic pride. In the long run, the new towns will be judged by the kind of citizens they produce, by whether they create this spirit of friendship, neighbourliness and comradeship.'

W.S. Morrison, replying for the Opposition, had been responsible for much of the earlier work on the new legislation when he was Minister of Town and Country Planning in the wartime coalition government. He congratulated Silkin on 'a speech of great clarity and eloquence [with] a welcome absence of any doctrinal persuasions or attempts to divide the House on party lines. After the Right Honourable Gentleman's description of the sort of new towns which he projected, one could not help feeling that they would be very pleasing places in which to live. . . .'[6] He and other Opposition speakers criticised some of the powers and procedures of the Act (dealing with the terms on which farms and owner-occupied houses might be compulsorily purchased, for example) but the Conservatives matched Silkin's enthusiasm for socially mixed communities, stressing 'the importance of having all the income levels mixed in a town, and not having the rich in one part and the poor segretated in another part'.[7] All parties could agree about the kind of world they wanted the planners to create — provided no one asked whether 'socially mixed', to become a reality, must eventually mean 'more equal'.

Silkin had temporarily united one of the most contentious parliaments in British history with a vision of the liberal dream shared by the coalition of interests supporting the idea of town planning — a dream expressed in a mixture of phrases ('a proper balance between the competing demands . . . in the best interests of the whole people', creating 'neighbourliness and comradeship') which stemmed directly from the utilitarian and utopian roots of the liberal tradition. To make a reality of this dream — to create a benign society, no longer divided by social conflict but united by common interests — it would be necessary to give people opportunities for having similar interests and for abandoning relationships of deference, contempt and fear; and that would call for much greater equality in life styles and social relations than Britain had yet attained. But questions of this kind and their distributional implications were not discussed in these debates. The coalition in favour of planning was no more than a temporary alliance of unequal forces; it had forged no lasting consensus.

Strengths and Weaknesses of the Tradition
In recent years, as this vision and the coalition on which it was based have decayed, many people have ridiculed its rather woolly naivety. Yet

its ideals were humane, and they had more pervasive and benign effects than many which inspired that reforming parliament. The new towns have actually been built, green belts have been imposed, and Britain has gone a long way towards eliminating both the savagely high and the wastefully low densities of urban building which still disfigure the cities of many other countries. Despite the havoc too often wreaked by urban redevelopment, thousands of beautiful buildings and hundreds of miles of delightful countryside and coastline have been conserved, wayside hoardings have been greatly reduced in numbers, and many of the worst horrors to be seen in other countries — the shanty towns, the grossest over-crowding and the more ghastly forms of pollution — have been prevented. High prices have been paid for some of these achievements: green belts around cities have increased rents and house prices within them; the new towns have proved to be an expensive form of urban development from which the poorest people have generally been excluded; wholesale rebuilding within old towns has destroyed a lot of small commercial enterprises; and controls on urban development have sometimes slowed down new investment or driven the investors elsewhere. But the good things — and some of the bad things too — were what successive governments intended planners to achieve. And to a great extent they succeeded: when compared with contemporary development in other countries — from the centrally planned to the freest of market economies — the environments which British planners helped to shape have not been the most brutal, the most squalid or the most unfair in their impact upon people. That is why, year by year, Parliament generally demanded more planning and planners, not less.

The weaknesses of this tradition are characteristic of its strengths. It is at its best in dealing with landscape — with land, and the things which can be created and conserved upon it. Sir Colin Buchanan summed up the convictions expressed in the Town and Country Planning Act of 1947 as 'the belief that the land of the country, after its people, is its most precious asset, not to be squandered, not to be exploited, not to be sacrificed for short-term gains, but to be zealously guarded and enriched for passing on to succeeding generations'.[8] He was speaking for a living tradition, for that statement was no mere rhetorical flourish. It comes from the note of dissent in which, virtually single-handed, he set about overturning the recommendations of one of the most massive programmes of economic analysis ever applied to a planning problem anywhere in the world — the location of a third airport for London.

If this is the central core of the British planning tradition, it is not surprising that it has been more successful in creating and conserving a finished product than in promoting more continuous processes of growth and change, more skilled in dealing with space than with time, stronger on architecture than economics, better equipped to make aesthetic judgements than to analyse how resources flow through the economy or how to enlarge or redirect those flows. Those priorities are unsurprising; they were the priorities the country expected of its planners. It was a country which assumed that the motors of economic growth would keep turning, and no special steps were required to create and foster productive enterprise, jobs and earnings, or to link industrial development to the development of housing, transport, education and other sectors of an urban economy. Only in the new towns did planners adopt more comprehensive and economically-oriented strategies — and it was many years before these towns made much impact. Elsewhere, peace, full employment and the 'welfare state' were expected to solve the nation's main social and economic problems.

Town planning was designed, in effect, to tidy up Britain's urban estate. Once the first ambitious aim of acquiring a large share of the profits of urban development for the community was abandoned, no radical change could be expected to occur as a result of town planning because no major redistribution of resources could be brought about without securing consents, step by step, from the local authorities and the central government to which aggrieved property owners had extensive rights of appeal.

The structure and deployment of the planning profession reinforced these tendencies. The élites of the profession generally worked in local government or in private practice on problems at the urban scale, rather than at regional or national scales where there was more scope for economic approaches to planning. At the urban scale the élites tended to work on problems of design, where architects predominated, rather than on development control where geographers were more common, or on longer-term development and structure planning where the scarcer economists and social scientists were more often found.[9] Planners' working relationships with people in the community were designed to meet the needs of solicitors, surveyors and other professional advisers of property owners. The press and the public were generally kept at arm's length. Only in the new towns did planners take trouble over their public relations.

Planners were expected to create environments which were humane in scale, built at moderate densities, interspersed with green space, and likely to foster neighbourly relations of the sort which were widely believed to flourish in village communities. Many of them were therefore hostile to big cities; they tried to restrain urban growth ('sprawl' it was often called), to get people out of big towns into small ones, and to make towns as much like villages as possible by balkanising them into 'neighbourhoods'. Those priorities too are unsurprising; they reflected the values of the British establishment expressed in Parliament (as we have shown), in the correspondence columns of *The Times*, and in the environment of neighbourhoods like Hampstead Garden Suburb, Richmond and Tonbridge where the establishment is thick upon the ground. A profession dominated by these aesthetic values was ill-equipped to cope with strategic big-city issues, unforeseen in 1947, such as a massive increase in wealth and population, the arrival of large ethnic minorities in overcrowded inner city neighbourhoods, the spread of the motor car, the demand for urban motorways, the decay of public transport, the massive outflow of manufacturing industry from the biggest cities, the office building boom and a revolution in engineering technology which transformed the whole scale of city buildings.

Despite its humane values and rather amateurishly sociological concern for 'community', the whole style of British planning was fundamentally élitist, as was so much of the liberal tradition from which it sprang. The planners' confidence in the benevolence of the social order and its governments was not wholly discreditable: the British establishment has not been merely paternalistic — it has often been genuinely paternal. Few market economies have gone so far in reducing the influence of the profit motive in the production and distribution of housing and medical care; no country has carried through so large a programme of slum clearance and rehousing, and few European countries have been so successful in avoiding harshly contrasting distinctions between a predominantly house-dwelling middle-class and a predominantly flat-dwelling working-class. The houses and gardens in which most of the British live are a significant social achievement.[10]

If British planners were socially complacent beneath their utopian enthusiasm, that was a characteristic they shared with most professions. Silkin's vision, warmly welcomed by Conservative MPs, of socially mixed communities full of 'friendship, neighbourliness and comradeship' expressed a widespread middle-class yearning for a society in which working-class people would become cultured, orderly and docile . . . middle-class in fact. The images in this rhetoric are those of the feudal village (but healthier, better educated and less deferential). They leave little room for big industry, big bureaucracies, and big buildings, or for trade unions, political parties, the mass media, mass entertainment, the mass-produced motor car and other realities of a modern, urban society.

The planning system created by post-war legislation was itself hammered out in élitist fashion, carefully shielded from overt political influences, in working groups set up by the War Aims Committee of the Cabinet established in 1940, the Cabinet Committee on Reconstruction Problems set up next year and other committees which followed them. In order to satisfy public demands for convincing war aims without upsetting the precarious unity of a coalition government, major problems were treated whenever possible as technical issues to be handed over to civil servants. Disputes within the Cabinet — bitter though they were on occasion — were kept secret, even from parliament. Inside the bureaucracy the protagonists seem rarely to have recognised the major social conflicts implicit in the debate about planning. Barry Cullingworth's official history[11] of these debates reports one of those rare incidents. It appears in a private letter by Lord Justice Scott in November 1943 to W. S. Morrison, then Minister of Town and Country Planning. He begins 'Dear Shakes' and comes straight to the main point which is to urge Morrison to ensure that 'Statutory Undertakers' are brought under the control of the planning authorities:

> the London Passenger Transport Board illustrates the danger. They deliberately made railways into *pure* country round London in order to create new traffic by creating vast new suburbs — which they called 'metroland' in advance. They did this all round London in many directions: at the same time they left old industrial and over-populated districts of London very inadequately served . . . it is a striking case of development forced *against* national interest or balance. Yours ever, Leslie.

Cullingworth goes on to say that 'Morrison replied in more sober terms to the effect that he was fully seized of the problem.' Such issues were not publicly discussed: only an inner circle and their friends knew they were being considered. A coalition of interests founded on tacit agreements to bury divisive conflicts of this sort was unlikely to last indefinitely.

The biggest problem of all — how to acquire for the community a proper share of the profits of development which accrue in the form of the rising values of land allocated to different uses by the community's planners — was handed to the Uthwatt Committee, characteristically entitled 'the *Expert* Committee on Compensation and Betterment'. Its Report,[12] like most of the main documents on planning, was difficult for laymen to understand, and the essentially political questions of the distribution of the costs and benefits of urban development were not publicly discussed. Wider public participation in planning was never seriously considered. Silkin himself recognised the problem, saying 'in the past, plans have been too much the plans of officials and not the plans of individuals, but I hope we are going to stop that'.[13] Little was done, however, to realise that aspiration.

To sum up: the strengths of the planning system of 1947 entailed corresponding weaknesses. Planners were ill-equipped to understand or foster economic development. Their professional imagination was essentially backward-looking and anti-urban. They viewed the world paternalistically and kept their profession and its policies off the hustings and out of politics as far as possible.

Why the Tradition Survived

If British planning suffered from defects which now seem obvious, how did it continue so little changed for so long? A certain social complacency and political docility were essential for the profession's survival. Planning of all kinds had been fashionable in 1945: 'We planned the war — we must plan the peace' was a recurring slogan. The Labour Party's election manifesto in that year gave a prominent place to town and country planning, promising 'a radical solution for the crippling problems of land acquisition and use in the service of the national plan', 'a revenue for public funds from "betterment"', and progress towards 'land nationalisation'. But planning figured hardly at all in Labour's manifestos for the 1950 and 1951 elections. In 1950 the Conservatives were promising they would 'drastically change the 1947 Act [which had proved] much too cumbersome, too rigid and too slow'. Next year they asserted more briefly that 'the whole system of town planning and development charges needs drastic overhaul'.[14]

For a while the term 'planning' itself became discredited and was dropped from the title of the central ministry responsible for it which was renamed the Ministry of Housing and Local Government. The few economists in the profession tended at this time to abandon it to the geographers and architects. The government designated no fresh new towns and treated town expansion schemes ungenerously. The attempt to capture and redistribute development values was discarded. Green belts became a consuming preoccupation of the Minister: indeed they were probably the main thing associated with planning in the public mind during these years.

But town planning survived and so did most of the planning philosophy of 1947 because there were fundamental economic and social tides, unforeseen at the end of the war, running in their favour. The rise of electricity (flexible and portable) and the decline of steam (fully efficient only in very large plants), the spread of the motor car and the telephone and the decline of public transport, the rise of service trades (which often follow the location of people's homes) and the decline of mining and the older manufacturing industries (which tend to dictate the location of people's homes) — these developments, together with the more general growth of affluence and the decline in family size, were leading all over the world to the creation of new urban patterns. Densities were falling and living conditions were improving in crowded urban centres; people were moving out from the biggest cities to suburbs and smaller towns, and a continuous network of urban settlements linked by many dispersed lines of communication was being created in place of dominant industrial centres with centrifocal lines of communication leading out through suburbs to a rural hinterland.[15] The country's great regional capitals — cities like Liverpool, Manchester, Glasgow and Newcastle — were no longer economically or politically viable: their production enterprises were going to smaller towns, and the head offices of their firms, trade unions and newspapers were going to London, or further afield. The people had been leaving the inner parts of these conurbations for years, often to commute back into the city for work. Now the jobs were going too.

Although the strength and implications of these trends had not been clearly foreseen at the end of the war, it was no accident that the planning policies of these years, encouraging lower densities and the decentralisation of industries and people from the great conurbations to smaller, newer, greener towns, accorded reasonably well with them. The trends and the policies were a response to the demands of the same human beings exposed to the same economic and technological changes — demands communicated both through the market place and through the political system. That does not mean that town planning made no difference: British planning policies have helped to produce clearly visible differences between the urban structure of this country and that of others. For instance, the range of densities, from highest to lowest, is generally smaller in British cities than in those of the United States, France or Sweden; and land in Britain has been developed far more economically for house-building purposes since 1947 than it was before the war, or is in many other countries today. But, as Clawson and Hall show in their analysis of these trends, the major patterns of settlement in Britain and the more densely settled eastern seaboard of the USA, have evolved in fundamentally similar ways, regardless of planning **and planning** policies. The decentralisation of big cities, the 'suburbanisation' of the countryside and the decline of regions depending on older manufacturing and extractive industries are to be seen in most urban industrial countries.

→ policie @ vlise yrs – encouraging
low densities & decentralization of industry
& people from greater conurbation to smaller
newer greener towns, –

2 The Coalition Breaks Up

The Turbulent Sixties

The loose-knit coalition of 1947 broke up in the 1960s; since then the British have not recovered their assurance about town planning. From the beginning of the 1960s urban development entered a turbulent period which posed problems for all concerned with managing cities and their public services. Planners and others did their best to rise to the occasion. Their first responses were purposeful and optimistic. But urban problems proved to be enmeshed in more fundamental weaknesses afflicting the whole economy. Town planners, powerless to contend with these weaknesses, lost much of their confident sense of direction. They were not alone: their morale reflects the confusion and uncertainty of the whole society in which they work. In this chapter we briefly trace this period of challenge, response and disillusionment.

In the 1960s many organisations found they were dealing with a more demanding public — and not only in Britain or only in the market economies of the world. Universities had trouble with students, police forces complained that people gave them less support, pharmaceutical companies were sued more aggressively by patients who suffered from their mistakes and more working days were lost through strikes. These changes have many causes, ranging from a collision between the inflationary expectations and the harsh economic realities of the times to the appearance of a new generation lacking the deference to authority which their elders had learnt from depression and war.

In each field these changes had special causes and took special forms. For a decade and a half after the Second World War, British planners had devoted most of their attention to new development in blitzed neighbourhoods or on green fields outside the cities. Because few people were displaced from either kind of site and those who would later live and work in the new buildings to be erected there could not be identified when decisions to develop were taken, planning could proceed in bureaucracy's back rooms with developers, land-owners, lenders and their advisers, without the public either knowing or caring much about the process. But by the early sixties the slum clearance programme interrupted by the war had been resumed and bulldozers were biting into the inner cities. Clearance in Britain rose from less than 35,000 houses a year in 1955 to a steady 70,000 a year from 1960. In 1955 there had been too little grant-aided improvement to record in official statistics, but by 1960 135,000 houses were improved with the help of government grants and that number would soon rise much further — to three times that figure by the 1970s.[1] Building licences were abolished in 1954, and a boom in office building and city centre redevelopment spread from London to every major provincial city.[2] A massive expansion of universities, polytechnics and hospitals followed, much of it competing for space in the same inner urban neighbourhoods. As motorways gradually linked the main cities to each other, the time came to drive these roads into the cities themselves: Glasgow, Birmingham, Manchester and other large towns were carved up in this way, provoking further conflicts. Planning could no longer proceed in a private, non-partisan, élitist fashion. It was increasingly clear who gained and who lost in the course of these developments, and who was taking the decisions. A succession of studies have charted the social conflicts provoked by urban redevelopment and renewal in Britain and in many other countries.[3]

The dispersal of people from the great conurbations to increasingly distant suburbs and the growth of office work and service industries in city centres led eventually to a reinvasion by young professionals and executives of inner areas long abandoned to the working-class. The Rent Act of 1957 made it much easier to persuade working-class tenants to move. Their housing could then be sold at greatly enhanced prices to the newcomers. The boom in the stock markets, coupled with the generous provision of improvement grants and tax reliefs for mortgage interest payments, helped the newcomers to buy. 'Gentrification', the term coined for this process, entered the vocabulary of the planning debate. Competition for urban space was dramatised by the arrival of unexpectedly large numbers of immigrants seeking to enter the country before the barriers imposed by the 1962 Commonwealth Immigrants Act and subsequent legislation were lowered. In boroughs such as Islington and Kensington, people soon grasped that arguments about whether to demolish and redevelop a neighbourhood, or to rehabilitate it with the aid of improvement grants, or to leave it alone, would ultimately determine whether its houses went mainly to the established local working class (who would be rehoused by the Council) or to the new gentry (who would buy their way in with the help of improvement grants) or to the black, Mediterranean and Irish immigrants (who would fend for themselves in the market). Planning was becoming politicised.

The established, local working class were in fact rehoused on a massive scale. But many were stacked in tower blocks: the number of council flats in England and Wales built fifteen or more storeys from the ground rose from 8 in 1955 to 3,426 in 1960, and to 17,351 in 1965 (almost the peak year).[4] The social division, long familiar on the continent, between house dwellers and flat dwellers was beginning to appear in this country. Even before one of them collapsed in a gas explosion at Ronan Point, the tower block became a focus of special hatred.

Meanwhile the rediscovery of poverty and deep rooted social inequalities which the 'welfare state' had been expected to eliminate focussed attention on racial discrimination, the plight of the homeless, educational deprivation and other problems which the professions engaged in 'urban management' were expected to resolve. But they had little power to do so. Housing, health and education administrators had powers to wield a good deal of capital expenditure, but all that the town planners could do was steer some of the country's economic and demographic growth into the places to which people could be induced to go — so long as the motors of growth kept running. Fortunately, in the early 1960s, they seemed to be running faster than ever.

Taken together, these developments were creating a more turbulent world than the planning philosophies of 1947 could readily cope with. Underlying them were other larger trends. The economic and social assumptions of 1947 were summed up recently by a working group appointed by the Royal Town Planning Institute. After the war, planners had relied on static master plans of urban development 'for at least three reasons':

> First, though careful projections of population growth were made, they could rest on the comfortable assumption that future levels were unlikely to be very different from those then obtaining; a medium or long-term plan to redistribute population was not to be complicated by large future increases in total population. Second, an economic 'steady state' was expected, with no great economic growth. . . . This explains, for instance, why forecasts of future car ownership were too low. Third, it was assumed that centralist powers of control were going to be effective: in particular, a good deal of residential building would be through state of local authority enterprise, and industrial location would be controlled.[5]

All these assumptions were dissolving by the mid-sixties. Births had risen steadily, exceeding offical projections every year for a decade. Economic growth, though slow by European standards, was faster than ever before, and more space had to be found for urban development and roads than was ever envisaged in the master plans. Many of the controls of 1947 had been abandoned and the proportion of houses built by public authorities had fallen from 80 per cent in the years 1945-50 to 42 per cent in the years 1960-65. In the future an economy oriented to consumer demands in international markets would be less predictable and controllable than it had been in the past.

A Hopeful Response

Britain's response to this rougher weather was at first a hopeful one. Under the Government which had promised in the election of 1964 to achieve sustained economic growth and put an end to the 'stop-go-stop' style of economic management, a National Plan was drawn up; an effort was made to get workers out of stagnant industries and to equip them with more productive skills; backward regions were given more generous grants; and backward industries were reorganised with help from the state. It was some years before the birds released by this programme for restructuring British industry came home to roost: we trace what happened in Chapter 5 of this book. Meanwhile Royal Commissions and public inquiries were set on foot to ask questions about many hallowed institutions including local government, the marriage laws, the public schools, the jury system and parliament itself.

Planning and planners played central parts in what looked for a while like becoming a period of reform comparable to the innovative years immediately after the Second World War. The advisory Economic Planning Councils, set up in each region in 1965, brought land-use and economic planners together at a geographical scale which was intended to provide some of the missing links between national and local planning. The succession of regional reports, that started with *The South East Study* of 1964[6] and to which town planners made major contributions, set new analytical standards and more ambitious economic and social targets for growth.

The profession recognised that the planning system set up in 1947 had hardened into a cumbrous form of land-use control. The development plans were incapable of focussing attention on the broader strategic issues of social and economic development. The whole system was confined within the increasingly obsolete boundaries of the old Counties and County Boroughs and clogged by a huge back-log of appeals awaiting decisions by the Secretary of State. The attack on these problems was launched by the Planning Advisory Group, a small committee of officals and professional planners set up by the Ministry of Housing and Local Government, which reported in 1965.[7] Their main recommendations were written into the Town and Country Planning Act of 1968 which replaced development plans with a two-stage system for dealing, first, with the major strategic questions (through structure plans) and, second, with the more intensive local action required for specific places and activities (through action area plans, subject plans and so on).

The Planning Advisory Group worked in a very private way, without commissioning research, calling for evidence or provoking public debate — in striking contrast to contemporary inquiries into housing,[8] education,[9] the personal social services,[10] and other fields. That may have helped the Group to secure prompter action on their proposals than the other committees achieved, but it also helped to preserve the élitist seclusion in which they tackled some of the essentially political parts of their agenda. The section of their Report dealing with public participation was revealingly entitled 'Publicity and Participation'. It called for 'an exercise in public relations [which would] make for public understanding of planning policy, [and give planning authorities] a new opportunity of winning public support for their proposals'. Before long the more articulate sections of the public were to demonstrate at Stanstead and other potential locations for the third London Airport, in Piccadilly Circus and Covent Garden, in areas through which many of the projected London motorways were to run, in central Bath and in London's Docklands that they were not interested in 'understanding' or 'supporting' planning policies but only in reversing them — and if they could not do that, they were at least capable of blocking them. The 1947 Act had established that two parties — property owners and government — must be satisfied before development could proceed. The public have now established that for politically sensitive places and projects and for areas inhabited by a lot of middle-class people (particularly therefore in the capital and its suburbs) the people who live and work in the area must also be satisfied before changes can be made.[11] The appointment of the Skeffington Committee, which reported in 1969 on public participation in planning,[12] was the Government's first serious attempt to come to terms with these changes.

The planning 'interest' in central and local government also played an important part in the movement which led through successive reports and prolonged debate to a comprehensive reorganisation of local government throughout Britain.[13] Town planners made some of the most cogent criticisms of the old system which had been devised in the last quarter of the nineteenth century and no longer matched the larger and more complex urban patterns of today.

For a while planners seemed to be poised for a new take-off. The new structure plans of the 1968 Act appeared to offer scope for a much more demanding interpretation of their task. More graduate courses were set up in response to growing demands from employers and students. Economists and sociologists moved back into practice and teaching in this field. New kinds of analytical thinking, derived particularly from economics, physics, operational research and other branches of applied mathematics, were contributing to a profession hitherto notoriously lacking in analytical rigour and testable theories. Massive sums were spent on obtaining data for studies used to validate transport plans: Stage 1 of the London Transport Study alone cost £1 million at 1965 prices.[14] In 1967 the government and the Ford Foundation set up a Centre for Environmental Studies which was to develop research on problems of urban development and planning in universities, polytechnics and research institutes throughout the country. These initiatives were part of a more widespread movement, in which the Institute of Local Government Studies played a leading part, for the improvement of corporate management in all local government services.[15]

Doubt and Disillusion

Yet despite these high hopes many planners suffered by the mid-seventies a loss of confidence and a growing sense that the public were indifferent if not hostile to them and their work. That was due partly to the more general crisis of morale afflicting government and the public service professions during this time of depression — doctors, teachers, social workers, policemen and others had somewhat similar experiences. But planners had some additional discouragements of their own to bear.

The reform of local government eventually carried through in England and Wales in 1974 and in Scotland shortly after was regarded by many as a disaster. The proposals of the Redcliffe Maud Commission which would have made planning a major function of powerful, all-purpose local authorities were brushed aside. Instead, planners and planning were divided between two tiers of local authorities, each rather ill-matched in scale to the economic and social reality of the urban settlements to be planned. Structure planning, confined to the upper tiers, was cut off from housing and much of the executive work of local government. Attempts made in response to the Skeffington

Committee's proposals to promote wider public participation in planning often proved discouraging.

Following advice given in official reports[16] and the inspiration of the Institute of Local Government Studies, many local authorities made ambitious attempts to develop procedures for corporate planning, but town planners' relationships with this movement were ambivalent. At first some of them made a bid to become its leaders, but their Institute now distinguishes town planning rather sharply from corporate planning and does not recognise training courses for the latter as leading to membership of the profession.

As the depression deepened, expenditure on new towns, new universities, city centre redevelopment and other major developments — the prestige projects of the profession — was drastically reduced. People grew increasingly critical about some of the projects already completed, and planners and architects became targets for a good deal of public scorn. In the academic and professional worlds there was disillusionment about recent lines of research: the mathematical models, it was felt, had often been misused or oversold.[17] The Centre for Environmental Studies, though it remains a thriving and active institute, is no longer expected to sponsor research elsewhere or to lead a wider intellectual movement.

Structure planners, after a euphoric start, have abandoned some of their larger ambitions. The rise and fall of these hopes can be briefly traced. The Town and Country Planning Act of 1968 was being drafted as the Milton Keynes Development Corporation were formulating the following 'goals' of their new town which was to be the biggest 'greenfields' project ever built in Britain: '(i) opportunity and freedom of choice; (ii) easy movement and access; (iii) balance and variety; (iv) an attractive city; (v) public awareness and participation; (vi) efficiency and imaginative use of resources'[18] — these were what Milton Keynes sought to achieve. Meanwhile Francis Amos, Liverpool's Chief Planner, was going far beyond the traditional boundaries of his profession to appraise the social health and morale of his city, ward by ward.[19]

The Greater London Development Plan provided the first opportunity for bringing this more ambitious approach to bear on the planning of a large city. Thanks partly to David Eversley and his colleagues, a more conventional transport and land use plan was turned into an attempt to shape the longer term social and economic development of the capital. This was described by the Panel which later conducted an exhaustive public inquiry into it as 'a prototype structure plan'. Reporting in 1973, the Layfield Panel of Inquiry reproved the Greater London Council for trying

> to do far more than it can do. For example, it assumes that its policies can alter settled population trends, and in employment it tries to forecast supply and demand for substantial periods ahead. . . . No policies by a local authority can effectually change settled population trends in the short term. . . . It seems to us that local planning authorities must accept that structure plans are, above all, documents which bring together what is known to be happening and which contain the most accurate forecasts, without their being distorted by hopeful projections of the results of untried policies.

The Panel went on to say that 'the GLDP Written Statement is full of statements of aims which do not mean anything because they can mean anything to anyone' − a criticism documented with examples which sound much like the 'goals' of Milton Keynes.[20] The London Docklands Study Team drew their horns in. Reporting in the same year, they rejected abstract concepts such as 'moving the centre of gravity of London' or 'restoring the balance between inner city and suburbs' and concentrated instead on 'real deficiencies experienced by individuals or by groups, to the remedying of which Docklands could make a contribution'[21] (problems like poor housing and unemployment, in particular). But their Report and its five alternative plans for Docklands' future were rejected as soon as the public were invited to participate in discussing it.

Next year the Department of the Environment and the Welsh Office summed up official thinking about structure plans in an authoritative circular. These plans are intended

> [a] To state and justify . . . policies and general proposals for the development and other use of land . . . including measures for the improvement of the physical environment and the management of traffic; [b] To interpret national and regional policies in terms of physical and environmental planning for the area concerned . . . structure plans represent the stage in planning at which such policies are . . . expressed in terms of their effect on land use, environmental development and the associated transportation system . . .; and [c] To provide the framework and statutory basis for local plans, which then in turn provide . . . guidance for development control at the more detailed, local level.[22]

Town planners, to put it bluntly, should concentrate on land use and transport − the physical and spatial aspects of urban development which they are trained and empowered to deal with. An independent study made at this time traced the evolution of the debate about structure planning, and suggested that practice might in future develop along more flexible opportunistic lines of the sort that city transport authorities and the Scottish Regional authorities were trying out.[23] General strategies of some kind were needed and should be publicly debated; but it was not clear what part town planners would play in the operation.

What could planners really do? As they grew increasingly alert to economic aspects of urban development, the economy itself failed them. In England and Wales the numbers of decisions made by local planning authorities on applications for permission to develop rose to a peak of 623,000 in 1973 and then fell steeply to 415,000 and 454,000 in the years 1974-75 and 1975-76.[24] For a profession which had assumed that the economic motor would always keep turning, enabling them to steer development in the directions they chose, this was disastrous. Planners' powers were mainly negative: they could prohibit development, but there was little they could do to stimulate it when the motive to invest failed. Some local authorities had already set aside sufficient land for the building of houses, schools and hospitals to cope with all foreseeable needs until the end of the century, and most big cities have more floor space zoned for manufacturing industry than their declining manufacturers are ever likely to use. Between 6 and 12 per cent of the land in the inner areas of Britain's four biggest cities is vacant. A recent study reports that 'the amount of land that has become redundant and is becoming redundant through the ageing of the industrial city, not only exceeds that for which development resources can be made available at the present time, but exceeds also the likely future needs of the late twentieth century city.'[25] (We explain in Chapter 5 why people have been so reluctant to invest in new plant and buildings, showing that this is unlikely to be a temporary recession.) Meanwhile the continuing fall in marriages and births has redoubled all these depressing influences, leaving town planners with less to do and less power with which to do it. As a profession they have been trained to steer the chariot of urban development, confident that the economy — the horse between the shafts — will keep pulling. But if the horse will only hobble — or lies down and dies — what then?

We have briefly sketched the development of British ideas about town planning over the past generation. The 'official' story — as it might be viewed from the Royal Town Planning Institute — can be illustrated by two examination papers. The first was the core of the examination for town planners at University College, London — one of the world's great planning schools — immediately after the Second World War. It appears over the names of two of the founding fathers

UNIVERSITY OF LONDON

Examination for the academic
diplomas in town planning and civic
architecture and in town planning
and civic engineering: 1948

PAPER I

Advanced practice and civic design

1. What are the main building uses which you would expect to find in the central area of a town with a population of a quarter of a million? Give your opinion as to which of these can be satisfactorily combined in one building, one street block, or one zone; and mention the disadvantages in convenience and amenity that result from indiscriminately mixed uses.

2. Summarise, in the form of notes and diagrams, the main principles which should govern building development and mineral working in the countryside. Include in your answer references to housing extensions in villages, improved amenities and services for the countryman, and 'the urban fence'.

3. Show, by means of diagrammatic cross-sections and notes, the desirable characteristics and dimensions of typical streets as they might be provided for in a development plan for one of the Metropolitan Boroughs. Include an arterial or sub-arterial road, a central shopping street, a local 'through' street and a cul-de-sac, among your illustrations.

4. What are the symptoms of 'blight' and obsolescence in a town or district, and how would you measure or assess them as a preliminary to redevelopment?

5. What scale of provision in respect of public and recreational buildings would you recommend for a new town of 25,000 to 30,000 people, growing up around or adjacent to a wartime industrial area which is being converted to peacetime manufacturing uses? Illustrate your answer by a sketch layout or diagram to show which of the buildings are to be located centrally.

6. Discuss the advantages and shortcomings of the control of the external appearance of buildings, under the Town and Country

7. Describe the main types of housing that should, in your opinion, be found in a large residential neighbourhood; and illustrate, by means of diagrams, the features to be emphasised and the precautions to be taken when incorporating them in a layout.

W. Holford
J. H. Forshaw

of the philosophies of 1947: J. H. Forshaw, who worked with Abercrombie on the plans for London, and William Holford who was already becoming one of the revered figures in the profession — designer of universities and new towns, to be awarded the Royal Gold Medal for Architecture, the Gold Medal of the Royal Town Planning Institute, a life peerage and other honours. Candidates were given little choice: four questions out of seven had to be answered, and these questions provided a pretty clear impression of the work of the profession they were entering and the values for which it stood.

Courses and qualifications have changed since then. The following paper, set thirty years later, was University College's nearest equivalent to Holford's and Forshaw's paper of 1948. It was the 'core' paper in the basic professional training course for planners. Two different courses are now offered to students interested in the field of town planning. One, covering a wider range of disciplines taught with less attention to practical applications, is not recognised by the Royal Town Planning Institute although it is taken by many who later work on town planning. The other, from which this paper is taken, is recognised by the Institute as part of the qualifications for membership of the Institute. It thus represents the more 'orthodox' parts of the curriculum. The paper draws on a larger array of disciplines than its predecessor. Only three questions out of fourteen have to be answered. Physical design and land use play less important parts than in the previous paper, transport a more important part. Economics, applied mathematics, sociology and public administration are firmly in the curriculum, and several questions call for an understanding of political processes or pose policy problems to which there is no single 'right' answer. The candidates of 1978 live in an open, plural society which gives them fewer authoritative assumptions to rely on and no consensus about their profession's functions and values.

UNIVERSITY OF LONDON

M.PHIL. EXAMINATION MAY 1978

TOWN PLANNING

Planning Studies I

Answer THREE questions

1. Discuss the proposition that the effect of a number of recent government programmes (particularly the Community Land Scheme, TPP's, Housing Investment Programmes and Inner Area

Programmes) has been to move us away from local government and towards mere local administration.

2. Who stands to gain, and who to lose, by the growth of corporate planning in local government?

3. Write a review for The Planner (Journal of the Royal Town Planning Institute) of any ONE of the following recent works.

    a. Fred Hirsch, *The Social Limits to Growth*;

    b. Alice Coleman's commentary on her Second Land Utilisation Survey of Britain;

    c. Cynthia Cockburn, *The Local State*;

    d. H.G. Richardson, *The New Urban Economics: and Alternatives*;

    e. The *Report* of the (Leitch) Advisory Committee of Trunk Road Assessment;

    f. The new *International Journal of Urban and Regional Research*.

4. Is it right (as seems commonly to be assumed) that in a period of negligible population growth no new designations under the New Towns Act will be needed?

5. What, in your view, are likely to be the main impediments to successful implementation of Structure Plans?

6. Is the study of the behaviour and attitudes of individuals of any relevance to planning? If so, in what ways? If not, why not?

7. Discuss the proposition that poverty is not specific to the inner city and cannot be relieved by inner city policies.

8. Discuss P.W. White's assertion that passenger transport innovations are gimmicks, diverting attention from the basic problems of providing, pricing, scheduling and marketing conventional services.

9. Comment upon the view of planning analysis that its descriptions are at best out of date and its forecasts just plain dangerous.

10. How should planning research begin to cope with the problems of analysis typical of a period of economic stagnation?

11. Discuss the extent to which councillors can play an effective role in local authority policy-making.

12. Comment on the recent suggestion of the House-Builders Federation that: 'planners should be concerned with general layout, density and housetypes and leave the details to the builder who is subject to the disciplines of the market.'

13. According to the Association of Metropolitan Authorities the present balance of consultation in development control weighs too heavily against developers in favour of the general public.

Do you agree?

14. Discuss the view that the acid test of the performance of industrial employment policies is whether they shape the real life decisions and actions of industrialists.

Can town planning survive as a separate and distinctive profession? And if so, what is it to do? Senior planners are themselves uncertain. The Working Group on the future of planning already mentioned, chaired by a past president of the Royal Town Planning Institute, were drawing their deliberations to a close as the last of these examination papers was being set. They concluded that a choice would have to be made between 'a number of options, ranging from one to several planning Professions'. After briefly reviewing the arguments on both sides, they said that 'a unity is required between all planners in professional terms. This could be achieved either by a single Profession with a divisional organisation, or by a series of Professions which are members of an "association of Planning Institutions".'[26] They said that the first of the 'basic principles on which to found a new approach to planning [was] the need to focus on the community and its needs . . . the effect of planning should be measured in jobs and homes and stable communities and life satisfaction. . . .'[27] But to do much about those aspirations in the cities which most need their help planners will have to gain some control over money, land, buildings and other resources with which to generate jobs, earnings and economic activity of various kinds. They will also have to find ways of linking local initiatives to regional and national economic strategies which may boost or blight local efforts. Some planners were already trying to do this, and academics were exploring the same issues — their teaching often conveyed in courses not recognised by the Institute — when in 1977 the Government published a white paper,[28] foreshadowing the Inner Urban Areas Bill, introduced in 1978, which was designed to bring more generous resources to bear on these problems. Meanwhile other services and professions were contending with the same problems. We turn to these in the next chapter.

3 Social Policy Goes Spatial

The Rediscovery of Community

While planners were becoming increasingly concerned with social, economic and political aspects of urban development, students of social policy, social workers, educationists and people of the kind that Vice-President Agnew once called 'the radical liberal establishment' were becoming increasingly interested in communities, neighbourhoods and space.[1] They recognised that they were dealing not merely with individual clients, patients, pupils and their families but with people in the setting of a local community and the neighbourhoods in which they lived. An early and vivid reminder of the importance of community came from Michael Young and Peter Willmott whose first jointly authored book was for years more widely quoted by planners and by social scientists than any other study of this kind. They concluded with a warning that 'even when the town planners have set themselves to create communities anew as well as houses, they have still put their faith in buildings, sometimes speaking as though all that was necessary for neighbourliness was a neighbourhood unit, for community spirit a community centre. . . . But there is surely more to a community than that.'[2]

These were not new ideas. They would have been familiar to nineteenth-century reformers such as the reverend Thomas Chalmers, Edward Denison, Canon Barnett and Charles Booth. But in Britain the institutions collectively termed the 'welfare state' had been designed to assure national minimum standards in place of the services hitherto provided by local government, local friendly societies and local charities. That was the recurring message of public inquiries, Fabian tracts and party programmes over two generations, each calling for an end to the variations, confusions and injustices which reliance on the local community had entailed. The demand for uniform national standards, or 'territorial justice', is now advanced in more sophisticated econometric terms but it is still a major strand of thought about social policies.[3]

Plowden report acknowledged indeed movement

A renewed interest in community appeared simultaneously in diverse quarters during the 1960s. The literature which records this revival includes the Plowden Report[4] on primary schools which called for educational priority areas where extra educational resources of all kinds would be concentrated on deprived communities; the Seebohm Report[5] which called for the concentration of extra resources in 'designated areas of special need', and the unification of social services hitherto provided by different departments of local government and henceforth to be deployed in area teams which were to include community workers; and the Milner Holland Report[6] on housing in London which called for a more comprehensive attack on bad housing conditions in 'areas of special control'. In 1968 the government's Urban Aid Programme was launched to provide larger resources for housing, health and welfare services, day nurseries, education and other services in 'areas of special social need'.[7]

Voluntary organisations were thinking on similar lines. Three reports sponsored by the Gulbenkian Foundation called for the revival of 'community work' and the recruitment and training of more staff to do it.[8] The Child Poverty Action Group, Shelter (concerned with housing), Gingerbread (speaking for one-parent families), claimants' unions (speaking for people living on social security benefits) and other new pressure groups together constituted a formidable poverty lobby based on local branches in many parts of the country. Meanwhile lawyers were recruited to centres, supported by statutory and voluntary funds, to provide free legal services for people in deprived neighbourhoods. There they have come to recognise that legal services offered to individuals (to help a tenant in dispute with his landlord, for example) will generally be conservative in their ultimate effect, however beneficial to the client concerned. To bring about more fundamental changes, lawyers must act for collectively organised groups such as tenants' associations, local branches of trade unions and neighbourhood action groups, and seek strategic judgements which will extend the rights of these groups and modify the balance of power between them and their employers, creditors, landlords and governments.[9]

Thus 'neighbourhood', 'priority area', 'community' and 'urban' became well worn in the vocabulary of debate about social policies, and town planners (who had been talking about communities since the eighteenth century when their founding fathers built utopias) met social policy-makers coming from the opposite direction (people now rediscovering community and the spatial aspects of problems they had so long contended with in aspatial fashion).

These developments were not due simply to transient changes in fashion or a swing of the intellectual pendulum. Similar things would not have taken shape spontaneously in different fields of public service, in different academic disciplines and in different countries throughout the world if there had not been powerful forces at work to bring that about.

The post-Beveridge, 'Butskellite' coalition of interests which created, and was served by, the slowly evolving institutions of the 'welfare state' did not share as complete a consensus as the coalition which supported the movement for town planning. Battles over pension schemes, housing policies and the reorganisation of secondary education were real enough. Yet in this field, as in the planning field, most people probably shared four fundamental beliefs. First, that the community should 'level up' the distributions of income and living conditions by bringing those at the bottom of these distributions closer to their averages; second, that rational inquiry and analysis, monitoring social conditions and reporting on the plight of those at the bottom of the heap would eventually gain the support of public opinion and move democratic governments to act; and therefore, third, that the state was the natural and principal instrument for achieving this social progress. Fourth, and most important of all, was the assumption that although governments would regulate the processes of economic development, succour the casualties of economic growth, and stimulate the economy or steer it in particular directions, the economic motor itself would keep turning – and so, too, would the motor of demographic growth which assured a constantly expanding demand for the economy's products.

These assumptions, as we have seen, were being eroded. The demand for a fairer, more equal society was more strident than before. It was in the 1960s that a new generation, coming to maturity since the pre-war depression and thus less impressed than their elders by social advances achieved during and since the war, came to form a majority of the electorate. They learnt from a succession of studies[10] that although health, real incomes, life expectations, academic achievements, housing conditions and other measures of living standards showed striking improvements for the population as a whole, differences between the social classes had not changed much. Research by the National Children's Bureau[11] on a large cohort of children born in 1958, a decade after the legislation which was supposed to create the 'welfare state', showed that children of unskilled workers were less likely than other children to be immunised or vaccinated, to visit the dentist, to live in a house with hot water and a bath, to have parents who made contact with their teachers, and so on. Policy-makers grew increasingly determined to get to closer grips with these problems.

Successive committees of inquiry then called for a heavier concentration of resources upon poor neighbourhoods, hoping perhaps that poverty could in this way be reduced without disturbing the rest of society. Later research was to show that the problem had more extensive ramifications and poverty was not as heavily concentrated in small areas as might appear. The most comprehensive analysis made so far reports that

> the degree of spatial concentration of individual aspects of deprivation is really quite low. Even with severe overcrowding, which is the direct indicator showing one of the highest levels of concentration, you would have to give priority area treatment to 15% of E.D.'s [Census enumeration districts] in order to bring within the net as many as 61% of households with this type of deprivation. If only 1% of E.Ds were given priority area treatment, only 10.6% of all severely overcrowded households would be given help.[12]

But that conclusion was reached a decade later.

The Labour governments elected in 1964 and 1966 — as much a product of the reforming enthusiasm of these years as its cause — promised to put the ailing economy right and to create a more equal society. But the July measures of 1966, imposed as so often before to cope with a balance of payments crisis, followed by the scrapping of the National Plan, the devaluation of sterling and cuts in planned public expenditure, made it clear that neither promise was going to be honoured. Public concern about small communities then took on a more radical note among people who sought to do what they could within, and for, deprived neighbourhoods regardless of governments — or even in direct confrontation with them. Others found in nationalist and extremist causes an alternative expression for their disillusionment with consensus politics, the radical liberal tradition and the London establishment.

The Community Development Projects

People in the town planners' and social policy-makers' worlds who were moved by these concerns came together in the Community Development Projects (or CDPs), set up by the Home Office in collaboration with local authorities in twelve deprived neighbourhoods, starting in 1969. There have been many rather similar experiments. The Home Office's Urban Programme is the most expensive so far. The Department of Education and Science's Educational Priority Areas programme was one of the earliest, starting a year before the CDPs. Those launched since the CDPs began include the Department of the Environment's Urban Guidelines and Inner Area Studies, the Comprehensive Community Programmes launched by the Home Office and taken over in 1977 by the Department of the Environment, and the Special Partnerships now being set up for 'the regeneration of inner city areas'.[13]

The CDPs were not the first, nor the largest, nor the most lasting of these projects, but they are worth special attention both because their analysis of urban problems was more challenging than most and because the lessons learnt from them are still influential — though seldom acknowledged. (The Inner Urban Areas Bill, going through Parliament at the time of writing, owes a great deal to CDP experience.) Their original aims were to study the needs of their areas, to focus public attention locally and nationally upon these needs, to help the public services working there to formulate more effective and more closely co-ordinated programmes and to give people living in these areas a voice in the debate and opportunities for doing things for themselves.

In many neglected communities remarkable things were achieved by the CDPs and the local authorities which responded to their sometimes unorthodox and disturbing interventions. Nursery schools, welfare rights offices, hostels for the homeless and other projects have been set up wholly or partly as a result of their interventions. Programmes of urban renewal and house building have been reshaped in significant ways. Links have been forged with tenants' associations, claimants' unions, trade unions and other bodies. Yet most people, and certainly the leaders of the projects themselves, would say that the CDPs failed.

Those who worked on these projects were not content with local, small-scale amelioration. They wanted to improve the living conditions and enlarge the opportunities and the self-confidence of the people in their areas, and to set in train a programme which would achieve similar things in many other places. Their pursuit of these more ambitious aims led them to two depressing conclusions. The two most important reports they produced clearly trace the evolution of their thinking.[14]

Their first conclusion was that the neighbourhoods in which they worked were an integral part of a larger industrial society, and their problems were the local manifestation of the decay of that society and its economy. They were not dealing essentially with problems of poverty — a formula which lays the blame on the neighbourhood and the people who live there. Instead they portrayed these areas 'as hard pressed working class communities suffering progressive underdevelopment in terms of industrial decline and the changing composition of the local labour force'. Three of these areas suffered 'the effects of decline in port-related industries', two 'the decline of textile industries', two 'the closure of mining enterprises' and three 'the decline of manufacturing industries'.[15] The decay of these local economies had been brought about over many years by the run-down of plant and machinery, and the withdrawal of capital which was reinvested by its owners in other parts of Britain and in other countries. The CDPs argued, for example, that the decline of employment in the Chrysler plant in Coventry could not be understood without looking at the policies adopted by Chrysler in plants all over the world.

The CDPs' second sombre conclusion dealt with government. After trying fruitlessly — some would say too briefly and ineptly — to gain from central and local authorities the massive resources needed in deprived areas, they rejected the liberal–democratic assumptions on which their projects had been founded. Government, they argued, was ultimately the servant of the interests and classes which dominate society. Notwithstanding their concern for social welfare — a very natural concern for rulers who must avoid scandal and prevent serious disorder if they are to retain power — governments will do nothing to disturb the basic structure of society and the economic order on which it is based. If you are seeking not just some extra nursery school places but a transformation of opportunities throughout a city, you cannot expect government to be on your side.

'Experience', said the CDP teams, 'led them largely to discount the value of attempting to influence policy and promote technical strategies for change in isolation from the development of working class action'. They 'do not have strong expectations of the national policy effect of their documents, and considered their main importance as generating a debate within local political networks and local administrative systems.' 'Instead of feeding local evidence about people to the decision makers in the perhaps naive hope that they will do something about their problem, we will concentrate more on feeding facts and figures about the cause of a problem to local people so that they can create the pressure for change.'[16]

Some of this analysis has been presented before. Indeed, right-wing analysts have stressed that urban problems have large-scale economic causes which cannot be reversed by local, small-scale government interventions. So what follows? It was when it came to prescribing action that the CDPs — like everyone else — became less cogent.

Unanswered Questions

First, we need to know what economic strategies to follow. What kind of city and what kinds of industry do we want? For whom will they produce, and how can we create such places? Suppose fundamental changes *are* made in the country's social structure; suppose 'the commanding heights of the economy' are captured; suppose the revolution itself: what then? If we do not have convincing and widely understood answers to offer to such questions, governments anxious to survive will go on propping up failing industries and communities and whatever the colour of the regime, the outcome would still be ineffectually conservative. Radicals have been too reluctant to formulate programmes for the future, saying that the working class, given an opportunity, will formulate their own. But a democratic people will not support movements which condemn the present society without offering any clear vision of a better future.

Second, as spokesmen of the deprived become clearer about their objectives they must consider how the people for whom they speak can gain influence. As the CDPs' analysis of the problems afflicting the neighbourhoods in which they worked grew larger — looking to the city, the nation and ultimately to the whole world for explanations of the economic crisis of capitalism — the arenas in which they chose to act grew smaller and smaller. Deliberately cutting themselves off from central and local government, most of the teams ended up by working with shop stewards in particular factories, tenants' associations on particular estates, social security claimants, groups of mothers who could be helped to run play groups or youth clubs and other microscopic enterprises — beautiful work often, but no way to change the world. How should reformers rebuild their links with power upon a scale which matches the scale of the problems they have identified? Where, in particular, will those for whom they speak find the resources for political action? During the concluding agonies of the CDP movement its leaders turned successively to the Home Office, the Social Science Research Council, and the Gulbenkian, Rowntree, Nuffield, Cadbury and Sainsbury Foundations — virtually a roll-call of power within capitalist society. It is not surprising the projects came to an end: there is no subsidised revolution.

Since the CDPs drew to a close, the answer given to these difficult questions by the most articulate spokesmen of the 'community movement' has been that they are building their links from the bottom of the political system with groups which represent the indigenous, local working class. Their aim is not to advise governments but to arm these groups with the ideas and information they need in order to battle for themselves in the political arenas of the nation. Coolly examined, and shorn of a certain romanticism about shop-stewards and tenants' leaders, that answer suggests that the movement may be laboriously reinventing the wheel — or, to be more precise, the Labour Party. For that is how and why the party was originally created, and it is still the party which dominates all the areas in which the CDPs worked. If it has failed, what went wrong? We shall not get to grips with the problem if we confine our thinking to simple models of class conflict.

Closer study of the most deprived areas and groups suggests it is no accident that they tend to be neglected — under any regime. The political movements set up to articulate the social conflicts of urban, industrial society have over the years gone a long way to secure greater justice for organised workers and their families. We should not be complacent about these achievements. Major differences in life chances still distinguish the different social classes — differences reflected in the heights and weights of school children, in morbidity and mortality rates and life expectations, in educational attainment and much else. But across most of the English-speaking world and in Europe, east and west, the well-organised and long established working classes are generally more affluent, more secure and better able to participate in the wider society than they used to be.[17]

The most deprived people of all are now found — as they always were — on the margins of the labour market, the welfare state and the political system. They are an ill-defined stratum, including workers in the least skilled and least secure jobs, newcomers to Britain (particularly those with a poor command of the language), one-parent families and some of the largest families on low wages, all of whom tend to be confined to low-priced corners of the housing market from which it is difficult to secure a good choice of jobs if you cannot afford to travel far, unemployed school leavers who have had no opportunity of acquiring rights to social insurance benefits or joining a trade union, and people (particularly women and immigrants) who work odd hours in ill-organised low wage industries. All of these tend to be marginal members of the social classes to which they belong. Too often the institutions, rules and conventions which protect the well established core of their class discriminate against those on the margins. They may be excluded from better paid industries by regulations (imposed by trade unions as well as employers) which keep out part-timers, home workers, people with dubious medical records and life expectations, and people who have not passed through the proper apprenticeships. They may be excluded from municipal housing by rules which give priority to those who have lived longest in the area, spent longest on the waiting list, and have conventionally sized families which fit the conventionally sized houses which are all that the authority builds.[18] When unemployed they have to live on supplementary benefit while more skilled workers get insurance benefits with earnings-related supplements, redundancy pay and tax refunds.

It is no accident that these people are often excluded from benefits which other workers receive. They are not well represented by the trade unions (who are naturally less enthusiastic about the unemployed, school leavers, housewives without a job and newcomers to Britain than they are about their own dues-paying members). They may also be forgotten by political parties (who naturally listen first to the well established local people who provide their funds, do their leg work and regularly turn out to vote). They are too diverse and ill-defined an array of people to form an identifiable, representable interest; school leavers, immigrants, housewives, pensioners, the chronically sick (but in each case only a minority of them) do not constitute a movement. The services the community provides for some of the most deprived of these marginal groups (for example, means-tested supplementary benefit, not contributory benefits; special housing for the homeless, not conventional council houses; prisons, not mental hospitals) may then meet their needs in ways which expose them to hostility and make it harder for them to gain a foothold in the secure and central areas of society.

We must not assume that people who live on the margins of the economy will all in time gain the protection afforded by its more central and secure institutions. On the contrary, keener competition and economic depression may hasten the mergers which produce larger firms employing fewer but more highly paid workers in more capital-intensive industries. Measures for the protection of employment may discourage employers from hiring anyone for whom they cannot guarantee a permanent job. Falling tax thresholds and successive pay codes restraining the growth of money wages may encourage well organised workers to lay increasing emphasis on the security and the fringe benefits of their employment, and to exclude the less well organised from these benefits. Thus the living standards and security of those in the larger and more successful enterprises, in the nationalised industries and public services may be enhanced by maintaining a peripheral reserve army of smaller firms and sub-contractors which offer less well organised workers lower wages, fewer fringe benefits and less security.

In the most deprived neighbourhoods, the peripheral people often form a large part of the community.

Closer examination of the more militant forms of community action so far studied shows that the people concerned have often been on the margins of the working class, doing battle not with the traditional capitalist enemy but with governments, often governments of the Left. The heroines of Jan O'Malley's 'decade of struggle in Notting Hill'[19] were often West Indian and Irish women and lone parents in conflict with the Greater London Council and Borough authorities. In his review of the struggles in the Cité d'Aliarte in Paris, José Olives reports that the militants succeeded 'almost exclusively in actions triggered off by attempts to evict immigrant workers from their hostels or hotels because of the demands of the renewal programme'.[20] Squatters, lone parents, battered wives and West Indians provide many of the models of community action described in Cynthia Cockburn's study of Lambeth,[21] and they too were often in dispute with their Borough council – a Labour council. Thus we must be alert to the conflicting interests of different strata and fractions within each social class and beware of the easy assumption that '*the* working class', led by skilled manual workers, will ultimately put all social injustices right. For the most deprived people, the labour movement (like the governments it has formed) is as much a problem as a solution.

The dilemma is a very old one. Charles Booth understood it ninety years ago when he said 'To the rich the very poor are a sentimental interest: to the poor they are a crushing load. The poverty of the poor is mainly the result of the competition of the very poor.'[22] Such news as we get today from the centrally planned countries of the world suggests that revolutions do not necessarily change these relationships or resolve the conflicts they provoke.[23] John Benington and his colleagues, one of the most thoughtful CDP teams, have said that urban, industrial societies *need* the adaptability provided by marginal workers, marginal land and buildings, marginal social programmes and marginal people.[24] Each can be brought into play or excluded according to the requirements of the economy's managers. The more comprehensively planned the central core of the economy, the more it needs these marginal elements in society.

All this may sound like an attack on the Community Development Projects and similar enterprises. On the contrary, anyone who explores the formidable problems they tackled will encounter the same dilemmas, and since they have been amongst the boldest explorers the dilemmas have been posed more starkly in their work than elsewhere.

This book will not resolve them but it may throw a little more light on these issues. Do towns with different industrial histories have different social and economic structures? How are these different patterns related to the opportunities and living conditions of their people? Do some towns do better or distribute their benefits more equally than others? Do particular groups such as manual or non-manual workers, unskilled workers, women or lone parents do better in some kinds of town than in others? And if so, why? These are the questions we shall explore. Later we shall ask what parts planners and others can play in creating or changing these patterns, and at what scale and through what institutions such changes can be brought about.

4 Questions and Hypotheses

Questions

We draw the first part of this book to a close by outlining the main questions to be explored in the second part. There are five of them. In the last chapter we showed that people concerned with a wide range of policies and programmes and their local administration have increasingly focussed attention upon the development and distribution of economic and social opportunities. These concerns form the context of debate about town planning and social policies.

(1) If we are to study the distribution of opportunities, the first question to ask is the distribution of what? We shall be particularly concerned with access to opportunities in the labour market — access to work of the sort which confers pay and a status of some sort on those who do it. We shall ask whether people are employed or unemployed, and in what kinds of occupations. We shall also ask about educational attainments, car ownership and the means by which people get to work, because they help to extend or restrict people's access to the labour market. People's skills and occupations go far to determine their access to opportunities in an urban society as Table 4.1 shows. The figures were assembled from official sources by Richard Berthoud who has explained their origins in his book.[1]

There are many other questions we would have liked to ask — particularly about the distribution of income and wealth — but data were not available on these points at the spatial scale we have chosen to work at. We have learnt a good deal about housing conditions and other characteristics of the towns to be studied, but we have not been able to relate this information directly to individuals. (We know, for example, that manual workers tend to live in towns where there is a good deal of council housing and we know, on a national scale, that they often live in this sort of housing. But we cannot be absolutely sure whether they do so in the towns we have chosen to study.)

Table 4.1. Skills, Occupations, Opportunities and Living Standards

	Managerial and Professional	Other non-manual	Skilled manual	Semi-skilled	Unskilled
	%	%	%	%	%
Male unemployment rates 1971	2	3	4	5	12
Earning less than £45 per week 1974	7	25	13	27	45
Middle-aged men with limiting long-standing illness 1973	11	19	20	24	33
Poor reading ability at age 11, Inner London 1971	7	15	22	31	38
In housing without exclusive use of bath or shower and W.C. 1973	5	12	12	18	21
Households without a car 1972	15	48	45	69	82

(2) We must specify the kinds of people to be studied and compared. Since we are particularly concerned with access to opportunities in the labour market, we shall focus mainly on five broad groupings of the categories of workers defined by the Registrar General for Census purposes, ranging from professional and managerial workers to un-skilled manual workers. We shall also be interested in a number of other groups chosen because they may be more vulnerable than most, par-ticularly the youngest and oldest workers, the sick, large families and one-parent families, married women with two or more children under five and immigrants from various parts of the world. For some of these groups we can only describe the places in which they live. For others we can say something about the people themselves. We could have made many other comparisons — for instance between people in urban and rural areas — but those we have chosen to focus on seemed the most important for our purposes.

(3) We must choose a suitable spatial scale for our comparisons. What kinds of place are we interested in — urban neighbourhoods,

cities, counties, regions or nations? We shall focus mainly on towns, defined by the boundaries of parliamentary constituencies (there may be several constituencies to a town), because they provide better data for our purposes. Ideally we would define these towns (or cities as we shall sometimes call them) in a uniform way by drawing boundaries round the residential populations which look principally to each of them for work, but the data we need are not yet available on this basis. The definition is a crude one but it identifies comprehensible types of towns which we shall group together in 'clusters' for much of our analysis. These towns are also worth studying because they are closer to the areas — indeed, many *are* the areas — served by local authorities, their planners and other public services, and they are therefore relevant to the concerns of those who depend on these services and the professions which provide them.

(4) We must explain how we intend to compare these places. It is towns, not people, we shall compare, and we do that in two principal ways. First, we examine the incidence of 'bad' things (like unemployment and not owning a car) and 'good' things (like having a job and owning a car) for each group of people to be compared, asking whether the group is doing better or worse in particular places than members of the same group elsewhere. If, in a particular type of town, all groups tend to do better than similar people elsewhere, we shall regard that as 'good'. The town is presumably a prosperous place. But this tells us only about the quantity, not the distribution of opportunities. Thus our second approach will be to ask whether the groups with the highest status and skills in a town do less well in relation to their peers elsewhere than the less skilled do in relation to theirs. If so, this suggests the opportunities in question are distributed more equally than those in other places. We shall regard that as 'good' too.

Towns in which opportunities are distributed most equally might be generally more prosperous or less prosperous than other towns. The least skilled people might do best, absolutely, in more equal or more unequal places. Finding out whether there are any consistent relationships at urban scale between the volume and the distribution of opportunities — between prosperity and equality — will be one of the aims of this study.

(5) We must explain our treatment of time. Towns change very slowly. Their present character is only the temporary outcome of a long history. Ideally we would compare the directions of their development over a decade or even a century. The direction and vigour of these trends would often be more interesting than the state attained at a

particular moment in time. If equality is the criterion, a town which is growing more equal may be better than a town which is static or moving in the opposite direction, even if the latter remains for the moment the more equal of the two. Unfortunately most of the data available to us throw no light on trends over time. Thus we shall contrast towns at the time of the 1971 Census from which most of our data are derived, but bring to bear separately — usually for the whole country rather than for individual cities — evidence about recent economic and social trends, using that to explain some of the urban patterns which emerge from the rest of the study.

We want to know how manual workers in general, and the less skilled and more vulnerable people in particular, fare in towns of different kinds — how they fare both in relation to their own kind elsewhere and in relation to other social groups in their own town. It might be tempting to throw everything we can discover about British towns into the computer, see which places do best and worst according to our criteria, and attribute their success or failure to the other characteristics we know about. But it would be unclear what, if anything, we had learnt, for such a procedure would give us no assurance that there is a causal connection in the relationships found between, say, a city's rate of growth and the level and distribution of employment within it. And if these characteristics are causally linked we would have no way of telling which is the cause and which the effect, and no way of telling whether particular urban characteristics can be reproduced in particular cities by introducing in these places other features usually associated with the desired characteristics. We would also have no way of telling whether improvements in one town can be achieved without making things worse in other towns. Each town may perform functions, good and bad, for the economy as a whole which have to be performed somewhere or other.

We shall make better progress if we first present some ideas — 'theories' would be too grand a term for these loosely related hypotheses — which may explain the patterns to be explored. Our data can then be gathered and organised to test as many of these ideas as possible.

A Conceptual Approach
If we are particularly interested in the opportunities which a town provides for paid work, we must ask first about its labour market and the jobs it offers. The stock of jobs in a town will depend on the industries which have grown up there over many years, and particularly

on those which export their products to a wider market. The industries which serve only the local population, such as most of the shops, hairdressers, public transport services, schools and general medical practitioners, will differ much less from place to place within towns of any given size. (In a hamlet a barber's shop may be an 'export industry' serving a population drawn from a much larger area, but in a city of a million people, large factories, banks and building societies may serve only a local market.) The town's industrial structure will depend both on past investment in equipment producing for a large-scale market and on the stock of industrial land and the infrastructure of roads, railways, power and water supplies, telephones and other facilities available at those sites to serve producers and link them to the rest of the world.

Next we must ask about the labour force and consider how well its quantity and character match the demands for workers represented by the stock of available jobs. There will have been for many years a continuous interaction between the demand for labour and its supply: industries will have set up in the town because it can supply the skills they need, and people will have come to the town, trained themselves in particular ways, and sought work or refrained from doing so in response to the opportunities offered there. Those seeking work will only be a proportion of the people of working age potentially available for work. Thus the characteristics of those in the labour force will depend on the demographic structure of the whole population and on their skills, and these will be shaped by the stock of housing available, local education and training systems, the trade unions, the transport system (which determines the range from which people will commute to the city for work), the supply of land for these purposes, local tradition and culture, and many other factors.

We have briefly sketched the factors at work shaping the demand for labour and its supply. There will be weaker but potentially significant links between the elements on each side of the equation. Land used for industry cannot also be used for housing, schools and other purposes. Houses, schools and the infrastructure of public services will be provided partly from the proceeds of taxes levied on local industry. Influences will also be fed back to both sides of the labour market from the interaction of supply and demand. Too large a supply of workers or too low a demand for them may result in unemployment, falling real incomes or outward migration which will reduce demand and prices for housing and for other goods and services, including the products of local industries. Scarcities of workers may have the opposite effects.

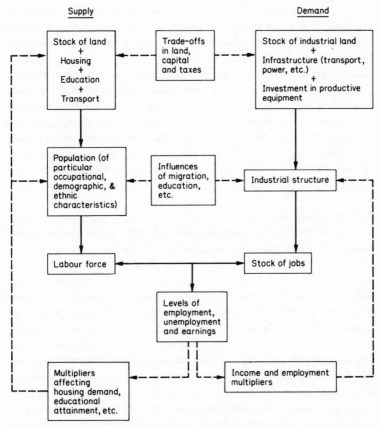

Supply   Demand

Figure 4.1 A hypothetical urban structure showing the main influences shaping labour supply

These relationships are represented in Figure 4.1 with the stronger ones shown in unbroken lines. All are hypothetical and it would be difficult precisely to distinguish and measure the influences involved. Influences shaping the supply of labour are shown down the left of the diagram while those shaping the demand for labour are shown on the right. Together they produce levels of earnings and employment which feed back influences to both sides of the market.

There will be frequent changes in the demand for labour and its supply. As industries and economic activities rise and fall, there will be changes, both nationally and at the urban scale, as productive activities originating in one kind of town (perhaps with innovative, high priced labour) come to maturity and disperse to others (in search of less skilled labour and cheaper sites perhaps).[2] If these changes proceed slowly enough, they will often be brought about through the normal turnover of the labour force as new recruits join and others withdraw from work, temporarily or permanently. More rapid increases in the supply of particular skills can be brought about by bringing more of the unemployed into jobs, bringing more people out of their homes into the economically active labour force, bringing migrants and commuters to the city from elsewhere, or transferring workers between industries or between occupations. Reductions in supply can be brought about in the opposite ways. Which of these processes will play the major parts in accommodating change will vary from one occupation and industry to another and from place to place. But in all of them the scope for rapid responses will be limited.

Some Hypotheses

It may be helpful to consider these processes more speculatively — though with less scope for validating our hypotheses — from the point of view of the individual first entering the labour market as a school leaver or as a migrant coming from elsewhere. His opportunities are likely to be greater if there has long been a buoyant demand for labour at places to which the town's housing and transport services give easy access. A town which has long been growing and is therefore accustomed to accepting newcomers (as workers, school pupils, customers, tenants and borrowers) may be easier for newcomers to penetrate than a static or declining economy would be. If it is to be a more equal as well as a more prosperous place than most, opportunities for work, earnings, housing and other things will be particularly concentrated in the central reaches of the markets for them, among the middle grade skills and income groups. Scarcities of these skills will encourage employers to train and promote less skilled people who might otherwise find themselves in dead-end jobs; and there will be ready access for migrants entering the upper reaches of the labour market. There the newcomers will help to prevent scarcities of key skills and tendencies to monopoly and excessive rewards among the rich.

That optimistic picture of a town's development reminds us that such a pattern of growth may leave other towns, which depend on less skilled work and tend to lose more of their most skilled people, more impoverished and more unequal than they would otherwise have been. Thus we must consider separately the effects which different patterns of development have upon individual towns and upon all towns together.

Upward mobility for workers already in the town's labour force is likely to be easier if the labour market offers an expanding, 'dense' and varied array of opportunities so that every worker finds readily available slightly better jobs which call for skills, similar to those he has already acquired, to deal with familiar situations at places not too distant from his home and previous work. Mobility will be easier, too, if opportunities in the labour market are matched by supporting opportunities in other sectors of the town's economy. It will be easier to get a better job if the education and training it requires are readily available. The job itself will be more attractive if it offers better pay, and if workers can find nearby the things they want to spend their money on — a better house for example, matched in price to their growing earnings, close to their work and the services their families need, and amongst neighbours with whom already they feel at home. If schools capable of giving their children access to better jobs and other opportunities are also within reach, the process of social mobility is more likely to persist from one generation to the next.

To assert the same hypotheses negatively: we should beware of *discontinuities within sectors* (industries demanding low skills and high skills, for example, with little chance for workers to move from one to the other) and *disjunctions between sectors* (industries, for example, which cannot satisfy the aspirations of an increasingly well educated labour force which is thus under-employed, compelled to emigrate, or deterred from high educational attainment; or a stock of housing which is ill-matched in quality and prices to the range of earnings generated by local employment.)

These characteristics of an urban economy will be most important for the town's most vulnerable people. Socially robust groups — highly skilled, mobile and affluent — can travel further and take greater risks than would be tolerable for more vulnerable people. We have been considering how people move on to better things, but for many it is difficult even to hold on to what they have got. A widow with young children to care for may be unable to work at all unless she finds a part-time job close to her mother with whom she leaves her children during the day. Immigrants with no savings, few marketable skills and a poor command of English may only be able to survive in close proximity to their kin, to particular employers, to retailers of particular foods, to special sources of credit and other supportive resources — their own mosque, for example. There is a good deal of truth underlying the folklore describing Jewish tailors, Chinese laundries and restaurants, Italian delicatessens and so on — small immigrant enterprises offering their own people somewhat sheltered access to the labour market in neighbourhoods where they may be patronised by members of their own community whose increasing prosperity can be recycled among them rather than being paid straight over to the wider society.[3]

For the most vulnerable people, large and sudden changes in urban structure can prove destructive. For them the collapse of a large firm creating massive unemployment, or wholesale redevelopment which disrupts communities by dispersing large numbers of people and eliminating smaller employers and corner shops may be disastrous. The social networks on which people depend for support in times of trouble and for access to jobs, housing and much else will eventually be rebuilt, but they grow slowly.[4] Larger towns may therefore have some advantages. People there are less likely to depend too heavily on one employer, one shopping centre or one housing estate, and the town is less likely to be transformed suddenly.

We have repeatedly mentioned the different markets in which people have to operate including in that term the 'markets' for education, information and other requirements of urban life in which money may not be the principle medium of exchange. The political market place can be regarded as another sector of an urban society, but it is a particularly important one because it is here that decisions are taken which may help to shape all other markets and the distribution of their benefits. In Britain more than nine-tenths of the schools, nearly all the hospitals, and one-third of the housing belong to the central or local authorities, and most of the remaining housing and many other activities in the private sector of the economy are in various ways regulated, subsidised and taxed by government.

So we must consider what kinds of city create a power structure or 'polity' which is likely to protect potentially vulnerable people. We can be sure that the present living standards of these people already depend heavily on central and local government. We should therefore be looking for political systems which tend to be responsive to the needs of manual workers, and particularly the less skilled and more vulnerable. Such systems should be open to penetration by newcomers and by interests representing those who might otherwise be neglected, and capable of exerting an influence on behalf of the whole community upon the central government which is the source of so much of the resources and powers on which local authorities depend if they are to achieve anything.

To sum up, a city which provides both good opportunities for the less skilled and more vulnerable, and a distribution of opportunities between socio-economic groups which is not too unequal may typically be a fairly large town with varied, prosperous and expanding enterprises demanding some training and a wide range of middle grade skills, operating in an equilibrium with a housing market, an education system and other sectors of the urban economy and without major discontinuities within sectors or disjunctions between sectors. There would be good opportunities for the least skilled to improve their status and living conditions through training and in other ways, and a plentiful supply of the most skilled workers (managers, doctors, senior officials and so on) in relation to the demands for them. Monopoly and discrimination would be difficult to impose both in the political and in the economic market places, and a large and thriving public sector would help to redistribute resources and to protect the most vulnerable people. The inflow of migrants with varied origins and traditions would be sufficient to create a plural society whose members learn to accept newcomers, and whose political leaders have an interest in gaining the support of minorities. This is an optimistic scenario, suggesting that the most equal city and the city which treats poor people best could be the same place.

Although we cannot rigorously validate so speculative an explanation of very complex processes, we will re-examine it in later chapters in the light of our data, bearing in mind that if this is indeed a sketch of cities with various desirable features, it does not follow that such places can readily be created, let alone multiplied across the face of the land.

Conclusion

Our discussion has been based on assumptions which are in a fundamental way optimistic. We have called in effect for ladders of opportunity which are easy to climb. But ladders imply hierarchies and inequality. Some would argue that if they are easy to climb up they will also be easy to slide down; and if they provide a comfortable perch, people may do neither — they and the economy will simply stagnate. We should therefore make it clear that we assume that most people improve their skills, their incomes, and their general living conditions if given good opportunities and a wide range of choices for doing so. We assume they are more likely to succeed if they are confident that the risks and penalties of failure are small and the chances of success good. We assume, too, that beyond a certain middling level of affluence a community's most creative innovators and managers will continue to do creative things without material rewards which greatly exceed what similar occupational groups receive elsewhere. But we appreciate there is an alternative point of view. Others assume that in general people do best when driven by fear of failure and the hardships it may inflict, and by desire for great rewards offered to the few who succeed. Our formulation of urban problems and their solutions will be more convincing to those who take the more optimistic of these views of human nature. We believe our findings provide some general support for it, but we recognise that the world is much too complex for either point of view to be universally true or false.

Finally we would stress that although the questions explored in this book are important, they are not *all*-important. Town planners and social policy-makers have become increasingly concerned about issues of distribution, equity and fairness. We have formulated our questions with those issues in mind because we believe they are central to the work of these professions and to the wider society. But that does not mean they are the only questions worth discussing, or that success in tackling them is the only criterion by which public services should be judged. A planner who creates or preserves a humane, efficient and beautiful environment has achieved something very important, just as a headmaster who leads a school of high achievement or a social worker who enables vulnerable families to cope more happily with their troubles have likewise done great things — whether or not they change the rest of the world, or make it a fairer or more equal place.

This concludes the first part of our book in which we lay out the questions to be studied and the hypotheses which will guide our exploration of them. The next part presents our data. It begins with a review of recent trends in the British labour market, followed by a more static analysis of urban characteristics, the different types of towns to be found in Britain, and their performance in 1971 according to the criteria briefly outlined in this chapter. Then we look briefly at education, and the careers of successful people, topics which throw some light on changes coming about over a period of time.

Part II

5 National Trends in the Labour Market

In the next eight chapters, which together form the second and main part of this book, we present findings about the labour market and the economic and social structure of towns which throw some light on the questions posed in the first part of the book. These questions are too ambitious to be conclusively answered in the scientific style of Part II. We therefore return briefly to the larger issues in the third and concluding part of the book in which we discuss in a more speculative way some of the problems posed in Part I.

In this chapter we trace the main trends affecting the British labour market between 1961 and 1976. We concentrate particularly on the decade between 1961 and 1971, partly because we have better data for this period, and partly because developments in these years set the scene for the next chapters which deal with the year 1971. In those chapters we look at towns, their social character and the structure of their economies. Then, in Chapters 9 and 10 we consider the impact made on different kinds of towns by the national trends explored in this chapter.

Introduction

For years low and falling rates of profit in British firms have led to low levels of investment in this country's industries. As a result they have been unable to withstand foreign competition. While Britain still had the protection of Commonwealth markets for her goods and a sufficiently large inflow of funds from banking and shipping activities, her antiquated industrial structure could be ignored. But those advantages have either disappeared or greatly diminished. Moreover, since the mid-1960s these problems have been complicated by a slower growth in domestic markets. British industry has had to increase or at least protect profits at a time when the most profitable outlets for new investment were being cut off. Firms have therefore been compelled to seek solutions to low profits and low productivity by closing the oldest and most inefficient plants, and by increasing output per worker through reductions in the numbers employed on many production processes. This has resulted in a drastic fall in the numbers of workers required by production industries and drastic changes in the types of work and worker required.

The total numbers of people at work have not greatly changed. That is because other industries, mainly in the service sectors of the economy, have expanded. But the skills required in the expanding industries have been quite different from those which have been cast off in the declining industries. That has made the whole readjustment harder. For their part industrial employers have been getting rid of large numbers of workers with particular kinds of skills and offering instead smaller numbers of jobs which often call for completely different skills, sometimes with lower pay and status.

In countries such as France and Germany which until recently had a much larger rural economy, modernisation of industry was brought about by recruiting workers off the land and from abroad. Britain has for many years had no large rural population of her own, and she cut back the inflow of immigrants to a trickle in the early 1960s; since then there have always been more emigrants than immigrants.[1] In Britain it has been women, rather than country people, that have been recruited to the growing sectors of the economy.

These strands of change in the supply and demand for labour are very complicated to unravel. This chapter attempts to trace the main trends.

1961-1966

The year 1966 represented a turning point in the current crisis. Unemployment rose by nearly 300,000 that year — roughly doubling in numbers — and, apart from a brief and slight recovery in 1972-73, it has gradually increased since then to its present level of about one and a half million. The immediate cause of this growth in unemployment was a deflationary budget — the 'July measures' of 1966 — imposed in the usual way to protect the balance of payments. But although the catalyst was a cyclical downturn in demand, the root causes, we believe, were more fundamental.

The Labour Government elected in 1964 was committed to modernising the British economy: these were the first days of the National Economic Development Council, the National Plan and the 'white heat of the technological revolution'. Employment was being cut back in those staple industries which were thought to have poor prospects for long-term growth — coal, shipbuilding and textiles, for example. Elsewhere, labour-saving technology, mergers and rationalisations were being used — with generous financial support from the Government — to raise productivity.

For various reasons these developments did not greatly increase unemployment before 1966. First, in all but some of the declining staple industries, the growth in output was sufficient to absorb the rise in productivity without a corresponding fall in the labour force. Second, employment grew on a massive scale in parts of the service sectors of the economy — in education, health services, central and local government in the public sector, and in service industries such as insurance, banking, hotels and catering in the private sector.

Some argued that the service sector of the economy (and particularly the public part of it) was diverting workers from manufacturing,[2] but this was a misunderstanding of what was happening. Of the increase of over a million workers in the service sector which occurred between 1961 and 1966, 95 per cent were women. Most of them were married and over the age of 35. The service sector of the economy expanded by drawing women into the labour force rather than by attracting them from manufacturing. And most of the growth in female employment took place among part-time workers. Whereas the total work force, male and female, increased by 5 per cent between 1961 and 1971, the total labour input as measured by hours worked, fell by 0.5 per cent.

Employers had to seek workers from new sources because labour was generally scarce and the more routine jobs in service industries are not usually as well paid as jobs in manufacturing, mining and construction. They did not rely only on women. The massive recruitment of immigrants to work in hospitals, transport, hotels and catering was partly due to the shortage of British born male workers during the years up to 1966.

Women and immigrants were used so extensively to expand the service sector not only because the jobs were worse paid than those in other industries but also because they were very different. Most service sector jobs are non-manual, whereas most jobs in production industries are manual. The largest occupational groups in the service sector are junior and intermediate non-manual workers, whereas the largest groups in manufacturing, mining and construction are skilled and semi-skilled manual workers. The growth in the service sector during the early 1960s called for large increases in the numbers of clerical workers, nurses, teachers and so on. Most of those who were losing their jobs were men — skilled manual workers from industries like mining, docks, shipbuilding and so on. Compared with the gainers, the losers were of different skills and sexes, and they often lived in different parts of the country. Thus to expand the service sector of the economy, new sources of labour had to be found: it could not have been done so quickly by merely switching workers from one industry to another. Even in the next decade, when labour was plentiful and hundreds of thousands of workers were unemployed, the service sector was still expanding by recruiting women and immigrants.

1966-1971

Between 1961 and 1966 unemployment increased by only 12,000, but, as Tables 5.1 and 5.2 show, between 1966 and 1971 it increased by over 600,000. There were various reasons for this dramatic change. First, owing mainly to the Government's deflationary policies, the average

Table 5.1. *Changes in the Supply of Male Labour, UK: 1966-71* (thousands)

Occupations	Employed	Changes Economically active	Unemployed	1971 Unemployment rate as a proportion of 1966 rate
Expanding occupations				
Employers and managers	226	247	20	1.63
Professional workers	75	81	6	1.74
Intermediate non-manual	165	173	8	1.42
Own account	128	144	16	1.55
Armed forces	1	1	0	—
Inadequately described	55	189	135	1.32
Contracting occupations				
Junior non-manual	−147	−125	22	1.60
Personal service	−6	−3	4	1.51
Foremen and supervisors	−15	−7	8	2.13
Skilled manual	−381	−265	116	2.42
Semi-skilled manual	−384	−344	40	1.82
Unskilled manual	−170	−112	57	1.79
Agricultural workers	−89	−89	1	1.23
All occupations	−543	−110	433	1.23

(SOURCE: Censuses of Population, 1966 and 1971.)

Table 5.2. *Changes in the Supply of Female Labour, UK: 1966-71*
(thousands)

Occupations	Employed	Changes Economically active	Unemployed	1971 Unemployment rate as a proportion of 1966 rate
Expanding occupations				
Employers and managers	72	73	*	0.90
Professional workers	17	17	*	0.88
Intermediate non-manual	166	163	−4	0.70
Junior non-manual	107	91	−16	0.76
Foremen and supervisors	6	6	*	1.06
Unskilled manual	2	−2	−4	0.74
Inadequately described	76	292	215	1.16
Contracting occupations				
Personal service	−43	−50	−8	0.79
Skilled manual	−91	−93	−3	0.98
Semi-skilled manual	−162	−172	−11	0.87
Own account	−37	−37	−1	0.95
Agricultural workers	−9	−11	−2	0.54
Armed forces	*	*	0	−
All occupations	106	275	168	1.61

*Under 500.
(SOURCE: Censuses of Population, 1966 and 1971.)

annual rate at which the nation's gross output was growing slowed down from 4 per cent between 1964 and 1966 to 2 per cent between 1966 and 1971. Despite this recession, productivity continued to improve. In fact, for the economy as a whole, productivity grew at a slightly faster rate than during the previous five years. Thus fewer workers were required to produce a slightly larger output.

The drive for better productivity was pressed onwards by a drastic reduction in profits. Company profits (net of tax, capital consumption and stock appreciation) expressed as a share of manufacturing output stood at 17.5 per cent in 1964, 7 per cent in 1970 and 3 per cent in 1973.[3] Because profitable outlets for investment were increasingly difficult to find, productivity was increased not by expanding output but by writing off capital — and labour too. The oldest and most labour intensive plants were closed, production methods were rationalised and the same output was extracted from a smaller work force by reducing 'overmanning'. A certain amount of investment did take place, but this was generally in capital intensive areas, often leading to the loss of yet more jobs.

In the private sector of the economy the restructuring of industry was frequently accompanied by financial reorganisations which enabled the largest and most profitable companies to buy out the companies least able to withstand the squeeze on profits. Production was then often rationalised by reducing the range of products, cutting back on duplicated plant, etc. Thus it is no accident that from the mid-1960s the 50 largest companies increased their share of profits at a growing rate.[4]

The state was not a passive spectator in these processes. To reduce unemployment it took various measures which by January 1978 were providing a net increase of about 200,000 jobs.[5] But it also played a major part in the restructuring of industry. In the 1960s, for example, more stringent financial criteria were applied to nationalised industries such as mines, railways, gas and steel which, as a result, were among the leading contributors to the shedding of manpower. Together, the three industrial categories which are dominated by the nationalised industries accounted for approximately 20 per cent of the gross losses in employment between 1966 and 1971.[6] The state also encouraged the restructuring of private industry by establishing organisations such as the Industrial Reorganisation Corporation, by taxing the employment of labour through selective employment tax and by providing redundancy payments and earnings related unemployment benefit which encourage workers to change their jobs.

A final and major reason why the growth in employment experienced between 1961 and 1966 was converted into a loss during the next five years was the reduced growth of the service sector. The expansion of this sector by over a million jobs between 1961 and 1966 was followed in the next five years by an expansion of only 150,000. The main reason for this change was the decline of the distributive trades.

The Experience of Different Industries
We will contrast the experience of different industries before considering national changes which have taken place since 1971. Most of the data for this section of the chapter, like most of that for previous sections, comes from the population censuses. After 1971 we have to rely mainly on figures from the Department of Employment which cannot be precisely compared with earlier data.

Table 5.3 Changes in Employment for Men and Women: 1961-76
(thousands)

Industrial groupings	Total employed 1961	Changes 1961-6			Changes 1966-71			Changes 1971-6		
		Males	Females	Total	Males	Females	Total	Males	Females	Total
Manufacturing Of which:	8,340	+88	+106	+194	-180	-271	-451	-512	-275	-787
Textiles	789	-9	-50	-59	-41	-108	-149	-47	-54	-101
Shipbuilding	236	-55	0	-55	-14	+2	-12	-10	+1	-9
Metal manufacture	624	-31	+3	-28	-53	-8	-61	-76	-11	-87
Clothing and footwear	605	-10	-13	-23	-16	-45	-61	-20	-46	-66
Food, drink and tobacco	744	+19	+27	+46	-35	-23	-58	-33	-21	-54
Mechanical engineering*	N.A.	+37	+17	+54	+8	-13	-5	-98	-22	-120
Services Of which:	N.A.	+58	+989	+1,047	-44	+186	+142	+268	+977	+1,245
Transport and communication	1,662	-73	+40	-33	-64	0	-65	-89	-2	-91
Distribution	3,159	-59	+187	+128	-123	-120	-244	+31	+83	+114
Public administration*	N.A.	-63	+76	+13	+47	+115	+162	+17	+89	+106
Mining and quarrying	720	-151	-1	-152	-175	-4	-179	-48	0	-48
Construction	1,592	+279	+34	+313	-214	-3	-217	+27	+20	+47
Gas, electricity and water	374	+30	+12	+42	-66	+9	-57	-33	+7	-26
Agriculture, forestry and fishing	827	-79	+24	-55	-133	-3	-136	-34	-5	-39
Total†	23,245	+217	+1,164	+1,381	-782	-2	-784	-327	+727	+400

Source: The figures in the last 7 columns are derived from the Census of Population by the Unit of Manpower Studies. They have been adjusted for changes in the Standard Industrial Classification. The figures for 1971 were derived by applying the industrial distributions applied by a 1% sample Census of Population returns to the 100% in employment figure of the Census of Population. The figures for 1971-75 were derived from the Census of Employment and are not strictly comparable.

Notes: **The figures for mechanical engineering and public administration were not available due to changes in the SIC.
†The totals at the foot of the columns include inadequately described and not elsewhere specified. That is why they do not equate to the sum of sub-totals above which do not include these figures.

Many analyses of the current crisis attribute the growth of unemployment to the decline of manufacturing industry which, it is said, has particularly affected men. In fact the loss of jobs in manufacturing was proportionately heavier among women (accounting for 74 per cent of their total losses) than among men (for whom it accounted for only 22 per cent of total losses – much less than the proportion of men working in manufacturing industries). Some of the main figures are set out in Table 5.3. The changes, and the reasons for them, vary from industry to industry. We will briefly outline some of the more important of them.

The main losses in employment took place outside the manufacturing and service industries which are the two largest sectors of the economy. If we add together the losses experienced between 1966 and 1971 in all the industries with a declining labour force to produce a 'gross' loss

Table 5.4. *Percentage Contributed by Different Industries to the Gross Decline in Employment, UK: 1966-71*

Manufacturing	
Textiles	9
Clothing and footwear	4
Metal manufacture	4
Food, drink and tobacco	4
Metal goods, not elsewhere specified	3
Other manufacturing industries	8
All manufacturing industries	32
Services	
Distributive trades	15
Miscellaneous services	11*
Transport and communications	4
All service industries	30
Other industries	
Construction	14
Mining and quarrying	11
Agriculture, forestry and fishing	9
Gas, electricity and water	4
All other industries	38
Total	100

*Approximate figure.
(SOURCE: Censuses of Population, 1966 and 1971.)

of jobs, then very similar contributions were made to this total by manufacturing, by services, and by all other industries: 38 per cent of the losses occurred (in order of magnitude) in construction, mining, agriculture and public utilities; 32 per cent occurred in manufacturing, where textiles, clothing, metal manufacture, and food, drink and tobacco were the main contributors; and 30 per cent occurred in the service industries where distribution, miscellaneous services and transport were the main contributors. These figures are shown in Table 5.4. Of these industries, only mining experienced a decline in output (the only others in the whole economy to do so were shipbuilding and metal goods), and this was a continuation of the trend of the previous five years. Employment in mining fell because less coal was expected to be needed in future, and the industry was therefore reorganised by closing the less efficient pits to bring about a striking 27 per cent improvement in productivity.

Other industries showed similar patterns. In agriculture, productivity rose at a faster rate during the five years after 1966 than during the previous five years. Far more striking was the 54 per cent increase in productivity achieved in the gas, electricity and water industry between 1966 and 1971. Here the discovery of North Sea gas, which does not need to be processed, and other developments in the production and distribution of gas led to dramatic reductions in the amount of labour required. Rates of change in productivity over the period are given in Table 5.5.

Table 5.5 Percentage Rate of Growth in Productivity, UK: 1961-71

	1961-6	1966-71
Manufacturing	19	18
Of which:		
Textiles	22	41
Engineering	17	22
Vehicles	29	7
Metal manufacture	12	4
Mining and quarrying	17	27
Gas, electricity and water	21	54
Gross Domestic Product per head	13	13

(SOURCE: *Economic Trends.*)

Construction was the industry which experienced the most marked reversal in fortunes during this decade. A gain of 313,000 workers between 1961 and 1966 was turned into a loss of 217,000 between 1966 and 1971. Output was still growing in the latter period, although its rate of growth fell from an average 3.7 per cent per annum for 1962-6 to 0.4 per cent per annum for 1966-71: so productivity appears to have increased very rapidly. However, these figures must be cautiously interpreted because the introduction of selective employment tax in 1966 made it much more profitable for employers in this industry to hire workers on 'the lump' — that is to say, as independent sub-contractors supplying labour only, therefore sometimes evading tax and insurance contributions. This data, which depends on people's willingness to report their occupations and industries to census takers, may underestimate the numbers of workers in construction after 1966. (But these figures are much more reliable than those of the Census of Employment which excludes the self-employed.) Perhaps the most dramatic aspect of the decline in employment in these four industries — mining, agriculture, public utilities and construction — is that 97 per cent of it was made up of male workers (588,000), the great majority of whom were manual workers.

The service sector of the economy was responsible for almost as large a proportion of the total decline in employment as manufacturing (30 per cent compared with 32 per cent). Employment fell in the distributive trades by 244,000, in miscellaneous services by approximately 126,000[7] and in transport and communications by 65,000.

The service sector is sometimes assumed to be governed by rules different from those which apply elsewhere. The decline of employment in the distributive trades, for example, is sometimes explained by factors such as slum clearance, selective employment tax and the growing burden of regulations and paper work imposed on small traders. Though factors such as these may be important, the major influence here as elsewhere is the drive to raise productivity by industrial restructuring.[8] Output in the distributive trades actually increased at a faster rate in the late sixties than before, although the 118,000 increase in employment during 1961-6 was converted into the loss of 244,000; this represents 15 per cent of the gross decline in employment, a larger proportion than that accounted for by any other single industry. (See Table 5.4.) As in other industries, firms were concentrating into larger units to reduce costs and increase profits.

Multiples, defined as those with 10 shops or more, increased their share of total turnover, reaching 40 per cent in 1971 compared with 35 per cent in 1966. They built larger stores and closed smaller ones: while the number they owned fell by 9 per cent between 1966 and 1971, turnover increased by 58 per cent. These larger firms are the only ones in the retail trade with sufficient access to capital and a large enough volume of sales to introduce labour-saving techniques such as self-service on a really profitable scale. Their lower operating costs impose growing pressures on the smaller shops. Already in a precarious position because of these trends, the smaller traders may then succumb to development schemes and tax policies, but these are only the straws which break the camel's back. Similar trends also occurred in wholesaling, where there were large numbers of mergers, operations were concentrated into larger warehouses, and mechanical handling and bulk deliveries became increasingly widespread.

The industries described as miscellaneous services, which include hotels, catering and launderettes, also experienced a dramatic reversal during this decade. In the first five years employment in this sector expanded by 244,000, but in the next five years it fell by 126,000.[9] Once again, increases in productivity were the most important factor as labour-saving and self-service methods were introduced in many of these industries. In transport and communications there were job losses in both halves of the decade owing to the rationalisation of the railway network. Of all jobs lost in the service sector of the economy, 50 per cent were for women, many of them in non-manual occupations. Transport provided the exception, for virtually all the people who lost their jobs there were men – most of them manual workers. The impact of these losses on the service sector is hidden in the totals by the counterbalancing growth which took place in education, health and central and local government services – particularly in the first half of the decade.

It is clear that most of the jobs lost in manufacturing were in the old staple industries: textiles (149,000 jobs), clothing and footwear (61,000). Food, drink and tobacco, other metal goods and electrical engineering also experienced a dramatic loss of jobs. Again, the major reasons for that were increases in productivity and restructuring. In the first half of the decade, women were gaining jobs in manufacturing at the expense of men. But, as Table 5.3 shows, in the second half of the decade there were 50 per cent more losses among women than among men – 271,000 compared with 180,000. Because there were far fewer women in manufacturing industries, the rate at which they were losing jobs was much faster than that for men. Of the total losses among women, 56 per cent occurred in two industries alone – textiles

(108,000) and clothing and footwear (45,000). Most of these women were doing skilled and semi-skilled manual jobs. In other manufacturing industries too, women were losing their jobs at a faster rate than men. But because they held a much larger share of the jobs to start with, men's losses were much greater in absolute numbers. The jobs lost were mainly for manual workers, skilled, semi-skilled and unskilled.

These are our main conclusions for the years 1966-71. Manufacturing was responsible for a much smaller proportion of the decline in employment than is commonly supposed, and that was particularly true for men. Most of the men's jobs lost were not in manufacturing but in the primary, extractive and construction industries. Among women the decline of manufacturing was more important because women were losing their jobs proportionately faster than men — and losing them in industries like textiles which were heavily concentrated in a few towns. So, having been used as an alternative source of workers in times of labour shortage, many women were being sent home again. In service industries the losses in distribution and miscellaneous trades were partly compensated for, statistically speaking, by the slower, but continuing, growth in government and the social services. But few of these new jobs were of the sort, or in the places, which were accessible to women who were losing ground in textiles, clothing, footwear and other manufacturing industries.

1971-1976

Data for this period are less plentiful. What we have appears in Table 5.3 and shows that new patterns were emerging. The rationalisation of the primary industries, construction and public utilities seems to have been completed for the time being. Expansion was taking place in mining in response to the rising price of oil. The major loss of jobs was now in manufacturing, and the rate, as well as the volume, of loss was higher for men than women. The service sector of the economy, particularly the public services, was growing again on a scale similar to that of the early 1960s. Once again, they relied heavily on women for their expansion. At the end of this period the Government committed itself to restraining further growth in the civil service and the expenditure of local authorities, so these trends will again be changing.

Meanwhile the supply of labour was, and still is, growing. Since 1971, there has been a steady increase in school leavers owing to the rising birth-rate of the period between 1956 and 1964. Although they are not its more fundamental causes, this and other demographic changes play a major part in explaining current trends in unemployment. They were recently summarised by Richard O'Brien, Chairman of the Manpower Services Commission.

> The main reason for the larger employment creation requirement . . . is that the labour force is expected to increase substantially between now [1977] and 1981. There will be more young people leaving school and entering the labour force every year from 1977 to 1981; the number is expected to rise from 671,000 in 1977 to 725,000 in 1981. In addition, it is expected that the number of married women looking for work will continue to increase. In 1971 there were about 5.8 million in the labour force, by 1977 this had risen to 6.9 million, and the 1981 figure is projected at 7.1 million. The result of these factors, and other smaller changes, is that the labour force is likely to be some 700,000 higher in 1981 than in 1977.[10]

In other words we shall have to find 175,000 more jobs each year to prevent unemployment increasing still further.

Changes in Industrial Structure and the Demand for Labour

We have outlined the main developments which are changing the industrial structure of Britain. We will take this analysis further and consider its implications for the demand for labour.

The British economy is responding, rather late in the day, to changes which are taking place all over the world. Any country which intends to keep pace with its competitors must constantly raise productivity and reduce its costs of production — in the service, as well as the production, industries. Meanwhile the expectation of continuing inflation has pushed interest rates, which represent the price of the capital required, to historically high levels. This has reduced the rate of profit still further. As a response various methods are being tried to cut costs and raise productivity and profit margins. Shift work, for example, is being extended. This enables producers to keep their machines working continuously, or at least for longer periods of the day, and reduces the amount of fixed capital required for each worker. Job evaluation is being increasingly used, not only to increase the pace of work but to provide more flexible job definitions, to eliminate some jobs, to reduce waiting times and to redeploy workers. Casual and part-time workers are increasingly used to cover peak demand.

Low pay and redundancies are often regarded as quite different problems, but they are in fact two more ways of solving the same problem — the achievement of a greater return on capital. Some industries can install expensive labour-saving machinery, reduce their labour force by means such as those we have described and pay their remaining workers higher wages than before. But other industries, either because the restructuring of their products or technology is not possible or because the necessary capital and credit facilities are lacking, cannot reduce costs in this way. Hotels, catering, parts of the health and social services and parts of retailing and clothing manufacture face difficulties of this kind. They survive by paying low wages. What may be achieved in one industry by replacing workers with machines may be achieved in another by contracting work out to low paid home workers. Women and immigrants are often the main sources of low paid labour, shift workers, part-timers, casual labour and home workers.

Another way of increasing the return on capital is to substitute less skilled, lower paid labour for the more skilled and higher paid. This process, sometimes called 'deskilling',[11] can be seen at work in the figures presented in Tables 5.6 and 5.7 which show, for men and women separately, changes in the numbers of workers employed in each of the occupations listed, with estimates of the contribution made to those changes by three factors: (i) changes in the proportions of men and of women in the occupation, (ii) changes in the proportions of workers in different occupations within each industry, and (iii) changes in the proportions of the whole work force in different industries. These we have called the sex effect, the occupation effect and the industry effect.

Table 5.6 *Changes in Male Employment by Occupation, and their Causes Great Britain: 1961-71*
(thousands)

Occupation	%	Changes			
		Total	Sex effect	Occupation effect	Industry effect
Employers and managers	+16	277	−32	302	−11
Professional workers	+33	195	*	105	94
Intermediate non-manual	+45	259	10	165	98
Junior non-manual	−7	−130	−291	123	33
Personal service	−13	8	−11	5	23
Foremen and supervisors	+5	23	−6	58	−28
Skilled manual	−8	−454	30	−274	−170
Semi-skilled manual	−19	−323	27	−304	−169
Unskilled manual	−16	−192	−72	−137	7
Own account	+12	115	−16	138	−39
Agricultural workers	−45	−146	−33	−46	−94

*Less than plus or minus 500.

(For sources and methods see note to Table 5.7.)

Table 5.7. *Changes in Female Employment by Occupation,
and their Causes — Great Britain: 1961-71*
(thousands)

Occupation	Changes %	Total	Sex effect	Occupation effect	Industry effect
Employers and managers	+32	105	32	45	22
Professional workers	+37	23	*	10	13
Intermediate non-manual	+35	277	−10	44	211
Junior non-manual	+19	582	291	140	103
Personal service	+24	234	11	11	188
Foremen and supervisors	+27	11	6	5	*
Skilled manual	−18	−112	−30	−45	−39
Semi-skilled manual	−7	−100	−27	−57	−1
Unskilled manual	+30	174	72	16	71
Own account	+5	−7	16	−17	10
Agricultural workers	+30	8	33	−6	−11

*Less than plus or minus 500.

Figures in this and Table 5.6 are derived from the Censuses of Population. The calculations of the three effects can be illustrated by showing how the 'industry effect'
on women's occupations was estimated. Changes in the numbers of women employed in each industry between 1961 and 1971 were multiplied by the product of
(a) the proportion of women employed in each industry in the occupation concerned
in 1961 and (b) the proportion of the workers in each industry in the occupation
concerned in 1961. Repeated for every industry, this calculation was designed to
show what effect changes in the size of the industries alone would have had upon the
numbers of women in each occupation. The figures in the 'effects' columns will
not precisely equal the total change resulting, but will show the direction and relative importance of the three influences compared. The formulae were as follows:

Let f_{ij} = proportion of females employed in occupation j within industry i;

q_{ij} = proportion of the work force of industry i in occupation j;

E_i = employment in industry i;

F_j = female employment in occupation j;

M_j = male employment in occupation j.

Δ indicates the change in the variable between 1961 and 1971

For females, the sex effect is

$\sum_i \Delta f_{ij}(q_{ij}61\ E_i 61)$;
the occupation effect is

$\sum_i \Delta q_{ij}(f_{ij}61\ E_i 61)$;
and the industry effect is

$\sum_i \Delta E_i(f_{ij}61\ q_{ij}61)$.

For males the effects are defined analogously; $(1-f_{ij})$ replaces f_{ij}.

The most striking contrast in Tables 5.6 and 5.7 is between the enormous decline in employment among skilled, semi-skilled and un-skilled male manual workers (falling by 969,000) and the huge growth in employment among women in intermediate and junior non-manual work and the personal services (growing by 1,093,000).

Contrary to popular opinion, the largest losses have occurred among skilled, not unskilled, manual jobs. Among men the main reason has been the abolition of the more skilled manual jobs *within* industries (the occupation effect). Changes in the relative sizes of industries (that is to say the decline of employment in production industries — the industry effect) have, however, worked in the same direction. But in terms of percentages the smaller size of the unskilled group means that the rate of decline of unskilled manual workers is greater than the rate of decline of skilled manual workers.

The picture is simpler for women manual workers. There was a de-cline in the numbers of skilled and semi-skilled workers and an increase in the unskilled. So there has been 'deskilling' in terms both of absolute numbers and of proportions. Much of this must have been caused by the decline in textile, clothing and footwear industries, where most opportunities for skilled work for women are concentrated. But there was also deskilling brought about by the substitution of unskilled jobs within industries. When the experience of men and women is compared, it is clear that in unskilled jobs women have been substituted for men, whereas in skilled jobs men have been substituted for women. Among white collar workers too, it is clear that the substitution of women for men explains most of the growth in female employment in junior, non-manual jobs — that is to say the less skilled of these workers.

'Deskilling', where it occurs, is usually brought about by bringing women into work previously done by men. We cannot give precise estimates of these, or the reverse, effects. The classification of occu-pations is so coarse that many changes — in the work done by staff of the increasingly mechanised banks, for instance — will not show up in the figures as a transfer between different occupations. Meanwhile the process of 'deskilling' has been partly counterbalanced by growth in the numbers of employers, managers and professional workers in many of the most skilled occupations. That growth has been largely due to occupational changes within industries.

Changes in the Supply of Labour

The effect on unemployment of changes in the demand for labour depends partly on the response of workers. The supply side of the equation presents a complicated picture.

Table 5.3 showed that the greatest changes occurring during the fifteen years it covers took place between 1966 and 1971 when the demand for men fell in all industrial groupings, and the demand for women increased only in services, and there at a much slower rate than previously or subsequently. Unless mobility between industries is high, the loss of jobs, particularly for men in construction, manufacturing, mining and agriculture, suggests there must have been a big increase in unemployment among male manual workers, a decline in unemployment among those women who could get into the still expanding service industries and a growth of unemployment among women confined to production industries in which they were generally losing ground faster than men. But Tables 5.1 and 5.2, which contrast the experience of expanding and declining occupations, for men and women respectively, revealed rather different patterns.

In all the expanding occupations for men and in most of the expanding occupations for women the numbers of economically active people offering their labour grew faster than the demand for them. This produced an increase in the numbers unemployed. For men the unemployment rates in every occupation were higher in 1971 than in 1961, but the increases in these rates were remarkably similar in both expanding and contracting occupations. The biggest increases affected foremen and skilled manual workers whose investment in a particular skill may make it harder for them to secure new opportunities elsewhere when they lose their jobs. For women the unemployment rates declined in nearly every occupation, but not generally at a faster rate in the expanding occupations than in the contracting ones.

At first sight, the labour market seems to work pretty well. But we would have to know a lot more before drawing conclusions about the human implications of these changes. Men lost about 1,200,000 jobs in their contracting occupations, more than a million of them in manual work. Yet unemployment within these contracting occupations only grew by about 250,000. Where did three-quarters of a million manual workers go? It is unlikely that many of them could have entered the expanding, predominantly non-manual occupations. What evidence we have suggests that for men there was little movement between the expanding and contracting occupations. The main change on the supply side was probably due to the declining male population aged between 35 and 55 and the growing proportion of young people staying on at school: there was a fall of over 300,000 in the numbers of males aged between 15 and 19 in the labour force due mainly to lower participation rates. That does not necessarily mean that these young people were all freely choosing a longer education: there was a sharper increase in unemployment rates for men between the ages of 15 and 24 than for any other group over this period, as Table 5.8 shows. Among the remaining sources of adjustment on the supply side was the early retirement of older redundant workers. The numbers of economically active men aged 55 and over fell, while the numbers of older women in the labour force continued to rise. Of these changes between 1961 and 1971 the largest was the fall of nearly 600,000 in numbers of men at work aged 35 to 55.

Table 5.8. Changes in the Supply of Workers by Age,
Great Britain: 1966-71
(thousands)

| | | Changes | | 1971 unem-ployment rate as a proportion of 1966 rate |
| | | Economically | | |
Age Groups	Employed	active	Unemployed	
Men				
15-19	−369	−311	57	2.80
20-24	182	265	83	2.91
25-54	−208	19	226	2.17
55-64	−78	−3	74	1.58
65 and over	−45	−46	−1	1.02
Women				
15-19	−353	−325	27	2.12
20-24	143	168	25	1.43
25-54	274	367	93	1.55
55-64	77	103	26	1.56
65 and over	3	12	9	2.15

(SOURCE: Censuses of Population, 1966 and 1971.)

For women there was a considerable growth in total unemployment, but a decline in the unemployment rates, for every occupation except foremen and supervisors — and for these the increase in unemployment rates was very small. The growing numbers of women who recorded themselves as unemployed for census enumerators were concentrated in the 'inadequately described' group. Most were probably new entrants and women returning to the labour market after long absence who did not yet have occupations in which they could be categorised.

The big losses of employment for women were in skilled and semi-skilled manual work in industries such as textiles, clothing and footwear. Yet there was a very small increase in female unemployment in the textile towns where these losses were heavily concentrated. This suggests that in areas where opportunities for work are shrinking a lot of women give up the search for employment and no longer describe themselves as unemployed.

Conclusions

These are the main conclusions we draw from this chapter. The sudden growth in unemployment which took place after 1966 was not due only to a temporary slump in the economy. It was caused partly by an increase in the pace at which British industry was being modernised to withstand foreign competition. Other factors such as the recession, selective employment tax and the Government's active support for industrial reorganisation played a part, but they were not the main causes of change. Reflation and increased investment in manufacturing cannot be relied on to put things right on their own: indeed, more investment may increase unemployment, at least in some parts of the economy.

Nationalisation would not by itself resolve these problems. Nationalised industries like transport, mining and public utilities have been responsible for a large proportion of the total decline in employment and others, such as steel and shipbuilding, will contribute more redundancies in future. To make any significant impact on the level of unemployment the restructuring of British industry will have to be planned with a greater regard for the workers concerned. If it is conducted largely according to market criteria which treat lenders' interests as paramount the process is bound to be destructive.

British workers are facing drastic changes in the types of work available. Many of the new jobs are of a sort which the present labour force will not readily accept. Women, and to a lesser extent immigrants, are taking these jobs. Yet women have often been the first to be fired as manufacturing industries decline.

In most analyses of this crisis too much stress has been laid on the decline of manufacturing. Similar processes are occurring outside manufacturing in distribution, construction, public utilities and elsewhere. Together, these industries account for a larger proportion of the total loss of jobs than does manufacturing.

But the real impact made by these developments on people in particular industries and places is mediated by other influences such as the transfer of workers between industries and occupations, the prolongation of schooling, earlier retirement and the movement of women in and out of the labour force. These changes often do not show up at all clearly in official statistics, and their meaning is difficult to interpret. Early retirement, for example, may be welcomed or deplored, longer schooling may be a blessing or a bore, and a transfer to less skilled work may be bitterly resented. The bare statistics of employment and unemployment, on which we focus in later chapters for lack of better evidence, are no more than the crudest indicators of the changing opportunities available to different kinds of people in different kinds of places.

6 Urban Patterns

British Urban Trends

The changes in industrial structure briefly described in the last chapter have helped to shape Britain's towns. Together these towns constitute a map of Britain's economic history, the character of each reflecting the part it has played in that story. There are manufacturing towns and service towns, and within these broad categories there are groups of towns associated with particular kinds of manufacturing or service industry. In the last chapter we saw that these industries rely on different kinds of workers; these workers tend to have different kinds of education, to live in different kinds of houses, to travel to work in different ways and to spend their money on somewhat different things.

Slowly but constantly, these patterns are changing. For our purposes the main trends in Britain's urban development are clear enough.[1] The first is the southward and centrifocal movement of economic activity from the older industrial centres built up during the nineteenth century in the North and in peripheral regions of the country. Some have argued that we are witnessing a return to something more like the regional distribution of people and prosperity found in Britain before the industrial revolution. The second trend is the decentralisation of the largest conurbations as, first, their people and, later, much of their economic activity move out to suburbs and smaller towns in the regions surrounding them. There have been lesser trends too, such as the growth of tourism and the movement of the growing population of retired people to resorts, primarily on the south coast and to a smaller extent on western and other coasts. There are also trends at work within particular sectors of the urban economy of which one of the more important is the disappearance of the private landlord, who before the First World War was the main supplier of housing to all classes, and his replacement by local authorities and by building societies and other lenders enabling people to buy their own homes. Before the massive slum clearance programmes of the 1960s, the towns which had grown most rapidly since the First World War had the better housing and the largest proportions of owner-occupied and council housing. More recently, the rebuilding by local authorities of some of the biggest of the older cities (such as Glasgow, Liverpool and Manchester) and the continuing sales of older rented housing to owner-occupiers (particularly in places like the textile and Welsh mining towns) have blurred this simple picture.

Classifying Towns

Already we are beginning to classify and to generalise — which is what we must do if we are to understand the impact these processes make on particular groups of people in particular types of towns. We could have used an existing typology of urban areas. But all classifications are to some extent subjective: their value depends upon the purpose for which they were designed. Thus we thought it best to devise our own classification to explore the questions posed in Chapter 4.

We assembled a great deal of information from the 1971 Census about 154 towns or urban areas in Britain. These areas are listed in Appendix I, and shown on maps in the next chapter. Some of them extend far beyond the local government boundaries for the cities from which we have taken their names, but 64 of them coincided with county boroughs or had an excess or shortfall of population amounting to less than 3 per cent of the county borough's. For them we were able to get further information from municipal sources, some of which will be used in later chapters. Of the 159 towns in Britain with populations within their municipal boundaries exceeding 50,000, 127 (or 80 per cent) are represented among the areas included in our study. As many of them do not coincide with any municipal entity, they should strictly be called 'urban areas', but we shall describe them as towns or cities, using those words interchangeably.

Cluster analysis seemed the best technique for exploring the questions we have posed. There are various forms of cluster analysis, but they all work by grouping areas together on the basis of their similarity in certain charateristics. Areas are shuffled and reshuffled between different groups until the members of each group are as alike as possible and each group is as different as possible from the others. A technical description of the method is given in Appendix II. Richard Webber at the Centre for Environmental Studies played a major part in teaching us to use this method, and helping us to prepare the data for the next two chapters.[2]

The computer package for our cluster analysis could use a maximum of 40 classifying variables. We decided to use all 40 and had then to decide how many clusters of towns to have and which variables to use. After trying 10 different cluster analyses, comparing our results with other research of this kind and consulting other people familiar with this work, we decided to adopt the 13 clusters used here.

To decide which classifying variables to use we had to pick those which seemed likely to represent the main relationships and causal factors that operate on an urban scale to throw light on the questions outlined in Chapter 4. We did that by drawing a flow diagram of hypothetical relationships between the various elements in an urban system (Figure 4.1), and testing the strength and direction of these relationships by studying correlations emerging from our data. As we explained in Chapter 4, the labour market is the main setting and context of these relationships, reflecting our belief that opportunities for paid work are strongly related, as cause and effect, to housing, education and much else. The labour force and the stock of available jobs interact to determine the level and distribution of earned incomes and the level and composition of employment and unemployment. Low incomes and high unemployment feed back their influences on both the supply and the demand sides of the system, increasing the numbers of people living in bad housing, in poorly accessible places, in areas served by poor schools and so on. They also affect industry through reduced demand for its output. High incomes and full employment feed back more positive multiplier effects.

This simple model was sufficiently comprehensive to help us explore various theories to be discussed in this book. But its first purpose was to help us choose 40 variables which would represent the main elements in the model. We had 317 variables from which to choose in the 1971 Census of Population which is by far the most detailed source of information about urban areas. We divided these variables into five 'sectors'. They were (i) employment, (ii) housing, (iii) transport, (iv) education and (v) demographic characteristics of the population. (Unfortunately the Census tells us nothing directly about income or wealth and we could find no other source providing such data for urban areas.) Within each sector we chose certain 'key' variables which were too important to exclude. For example, the town's industrial structure and the socio-economic groups of workers employed in these industries provided key sets of variables in the employment sector, and their importance was confirmed by their high correlation with nearly every other variable in the system. We then eliminated all the variables which, being closely correlated with the key variables, conveyed little fresh information. Finally we experimented with a shorter list of variables by producing 10 different cluster analyses and choosing the 40 variables which gave us what seemed the most revealing results. They are listed in Appendix III. Researchers interested in other questions might have chosen different variables. In later chapters we have used other variables, not included in this list, to throw light on particular features of the clusters formed with these 40 variables.

Urban Patterns

Before considering individual cities we sought a better understanding of the relationships between the 40 variables which represent their main characteristics. We explored these relationships by examining the scores for one variable at a time for all 154 cities and discovering which of the other 39 variables was most closely correlated, either positively or negatively, with the variable being examined. In this way we traced the links which together form the network illustrated in Figure 6.1. They fall into ten groups or 'dimensions' which broadly support many of the general assumptions about the ways in which urban economies work which were outlined in Chapter 4. These dimensions are worth noting because they distinguish the clusters of cities which we describe in the next chapter. The strength of the correlations between each variable and its closest neighbours is represented by the number of lines linking them. The direction of the correlation between two variables is positive, and represented by two circles or by two squares at each end of the link, when high figures for one variable tend to coincide with high figures for the other, and low figures with low. It is negative, and represented by a square and a circle, when high figures for one coincide with low figures for the other.

The two central dimensions of this network, linked by the strongest correlations, deal with social status and industrial structure. The first of these, running vertically down the spine of Figure 6.1, describes the social status of a town's population. Its strong positive correlations link the proportion of people in the professional and managerial occupations, the proportion of workers with degrees and 'A' levels, and the proportion owning more than one car. There are strong negative correlations between some of these variables and the proportion of workers in unskilled and semi-skilled jobs, the proportion travelling to work by bus and the proportion of economically active women in the 15-19 age group — the early school leavers. This status dimension is probably the most important one distinguishing the clusters of cities described in the next chapter. It is presented separately in an enlarged form in Figure 6.2.

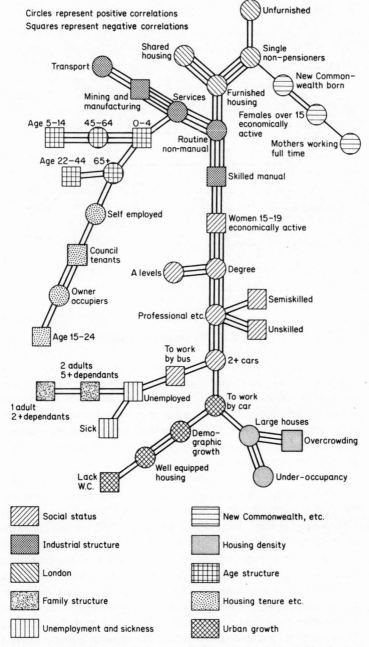

Figure 6.1 Linkage analysis: correlations among 40 variables in 154 urban areas

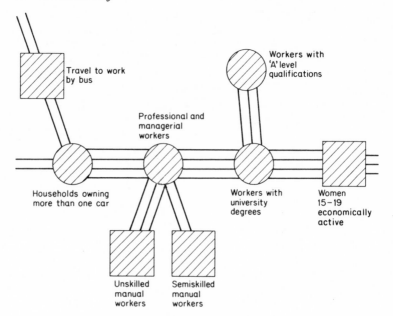

Figure 6.2   The social status dimension

Directly above this group of variables and turning 'northwestwards' is another which may be described as an industrial structure dimension. It is enlarged in Figure 6.3. All the variables representing industrial structure are included in it. Perhaps the most interesting feature of this group is the sharp contrast between the towns with mining and manufacturing industries, and the towns with many people in service industries. Connected with this is an equally strong negative correlation between the skilled manual workers and the intermediate and junior non-manual workers. The skilled manual and more routine non-manual occupational groupings are related negatively to each other because they are heavily concentrated in two industrial sectors (mining and manufacturing for the former, and service industries for the latter) which tend to concentrate in different towns. The towns with a lot of service jobs tend to have large numbers of workers in the more routine non-manual employment and small numbers in skilled manual jobs. Manufacturing and mining towns take the opposite pattern. There are few towns which have an average balance of service and of manufacturing industries. The strongest relationship of the semi-skilled and

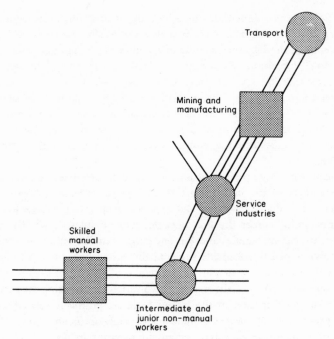

Figure 6.3 The industrial structure dimension

Notes to Figures 6.1, 6.2 and 6.3

The strength of the correlations between variables is shown by the number of lines linking them, according to the following scale:

Number of lines	R^2 plus or minus
1	0.55-0.64
2	0.65-0.74
3	0.75-0.84
4	0.85-0.94
5	0.95-1.00

---

unskilled manual workers — a negative one — is with the professional and managerial workers, but that does not appear to be so directly related to differences in industrial structure, and it is not quite so strong as the negative relationship between skilled manual and routine non-manual workers. These relationships are crucial to an understanding of the urban system as portrayed by the cluster analysis, and to an understanding of unemployment and other urban problems.

The remaining dimensions may be thought of as offshoots from the strong central trunk linking the first two. Continuing 'northwards' from the centre of the diagram is a group of variables which might be called the 'London' dimension because it so clearly distinguishes the special characteristics of London (and Cambridge) which form a separate cluster of towns. These characteristics are high proportions of shared dwellings, furnished rented accommodation, single non-pensioner households and unfurnished rented accommodation. They distinguish cities with large 'rooming house' areas and a lot of mobile young people.

Occupying more peripheral positions at the bottom left and the top right corners of the network are three dimensions which indicate the presence of vulnerable groups and deprived people. In the lower left or 'southwestern' corner the link between two variables shows that the larger two-parent families and the one-parent families tend to be found in the same places. Alongside the next dimension links unemployment and sickness: towns with a lot of one tend to have a lot of the other. In the top right corner of the network two variables measuring the extent of female participation in the labour force are positively related with the proportion of New Commonwealth citizens in the area. That dimension might be expected — many immigrant families would find it hard to survive without two incomes — but it is interesting to find that it is not related to the two previous dimensions of deprivation and vulnerability: New Commonwealth immigrants are not heavily concentrated in areas where there is unemployment, sickness, large families or one-parent families. That, however, may be a statistical illusion arising from the fact that so many of these immigrants live in Greater London — as we explain below.

In the bottom right or 'southeastern' corner of the network there is a dimension which represents the size of dwellings and the density at which houses are occupied. This suggests that at the level of over 1.5 persons per room dwelling size is a more important determinant of overcrowding than family size. (At the lower level of over one person per room, family size seems more important.)

In the upper left side there is a dimension which describes the age structure of people in the town. The interesting feature to emerge from this is that there is a negative correlation between all ages up to 45 and those over 45. This suggests that the growing towns have a generally young population and the declining towns an older one, because migrants tend to be younger and thus more fertile than the less mobile people left in declining places.

Running down the left side of the network there is another housing dimension showing a negative correlation between the proportions of owner-occupied houses and council houses. Finally, at the bottom of the network, there is a dimension showing, not surprisingly, that in towns which have grown rapidly many people travel to work by car, and their houses tend to be modern and well equipped.

Status, Vulnerability and Deprivation

Thus far we have shown only the most important links between the 40 variables which describe our towns — the simplest and most dominant patterns. We can use this evidence to answer four more specific questions. (1) Do people showing various signs of high status tend to concentrate in the same towns? (Our evidence shows they do.) (2) Do the more vulnerable groups also tend to concentrate in the same towns? (We show that some, but not all, do.) (3) Are various measures of deprivation concentrated in the same towns? (We show they are.) (4) Do the people with high status concentrate in the least deprived places, and the vulnerable in the most deprived? (We show that towns having a lot of people with high status show little deprivation, but that the relationships between deprivation and concentrations of the more vulnerable people is more complex and irregular.) The evidence to support these brief answers to complicated questions follows.

(1) High status

We used four indicators of the presence of 'high status' people in a town. They were the percentages of:

(a) Professional and managerial workers in the labour force (we will call this indicator 'professional' for short);
(b) Workers with a university degree (degree);
(c) Households with more than one car (>1 car); and
(d) Households in houses with unshared use of bath, inside toilet, and hot water (exclusive amenities — described in Figure 6.1 as 'well-equipped housing').

The correlations between these indicators, showing the extent to which they tend to concentrate in the same towns, appear in Table 6.1. In the small network diagrams below each table we have distinguished only the strongest links between variables, and only those outside the range from -0.50 to +0.50. The meaning of the lines linking variables is as follows:

Number of lines	R^2 plus or minus
1	0.50-0.59
2	0.60-0.69
3	0.70-0.79
4	0.80-0.89
5	0.90-0.99

Table 6.1. Correlation Matrix between Indicators of High Status

	Professional	Degree	More than one car	Exclusive amenities
Professional	1.00			
Degree	0.904	1.00		
>1 car	0.883	0.776	1.00	
Exclusive amenities	0.481	0.419	0.556	1.00

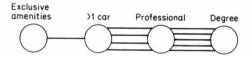

The main links in this matrix can be represented thus. They show that towns with high concentrations of one indicator of status tend to have high concentrations of the others, but those directly representing education, wealth, and status in the labour market are the most strongly linked. Two generations of council building for working class families must have greatly weakened, but they have not eliminated, the link between high status and well-equipped housing.

(2) The vulnerable

We had seven indicators of the presence of potentially vulnerable groups. They were the percentages of:

(a)   Unskilled workers (Unsk);

(b)   Large families having 2 adults and 5 or more dependent children (2A 5dep);

(c)   One-parent families having one adult and 2 or more dependent children (1A 2dep);

(d)   People born in the New Commonwealth (N.C.Born);

(e)   People in the 15-24 age group (15-24);

(f)   People in the 45-64 age group (45-64); and

(g)   People aged 65 or more (65+).

There is some evidence that older and younger workers are more vulnerable than are those in the prime of life to unemployment, to industrial changes which make their skills obsolete and to other hazards of the labour market — which is why we distinguished groups (e), (f) and (g) in this list.

Table 6.2 Correlation Matrix between Indicators of Vulnerability

	Unsk.	2A 5dep.	1A 2dep.	N.C.Born	15-24	54-64	65+
Unsk.	1.00						
2A 5dep.	0.617	1.00					
1A 2dep.	0.572	0.695	1.00				
N.C.Born	-0.206	-0.027	0.126	1.00			
15-24	0.536	0.470	0.517	0.277	1.00		
45-64	-0.128	-0.384	-0.186	0.302	-0.187	1.00	
65+	-0.139	-0.372	-0.147	-0.064	-0.444	0.602	1.00

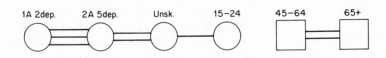

This network shows that the distribution of potentially vulnerable people is more complicated than that of high status people. High proportions of the unskilled, large families, one-parent families and young workers — the unemployment-prone 15-24 age group — tend to be concentrated in the same towns. These tend to be the classic victims of working class poverty. High concentrations of older workers and pensioners — the age groups over 45 — also tend to go together, but they are not concentrated particularly heavily in the towns with other vulnerable groups. Those born in the New Commonwealth are not heavily concentrated in either kind of town, but they are somewhat more common in towns with older workers and less common in towns with many large families and unskilled workers. Table 10.1 on page 135 presents these patterns for all clusters of towns. If these figures suggest that immigrants are not concentrated in deprived areas, they may be misleading. Those born in the New Commonwealth countries are concentrated particularly heavily in London. Since we have defined London as the Greater London Council area, it probably appears a good deal more prosperous than are the parts of it where immigrants actually live.

(3) Deprivation

We had eight indicators of deprivation. They were the percentages of:

(a)   Unskilled workers — an indicator also used to represent vulnerability (Unsk);

(b)   Unemployed workers (Unemp);

(c)   Workers unable to work owing to illness (Sick);

(d)   Married women with 2 or more children under five working 30 hours or more a week (M.W.30);

(e)   Households living in houses without an inside W.C. (No W.C.);

(f)   Households living at a density of 1.5 persons per room or more (1.5 PPR);

(g)   Single women aged 15-19 who are economically active — i.e. working, unemployed or sick (S.W.15-19); and

(h)   Workers with 'A' level qualifications (A levels).

Most of these indicators are obvious choices, but some call for an explanation. We included (d) because it has been argued that, given the lack of nursery facilities, many of the married women who work full-time when they have two or more children under compulsory school age will be doing that to save their families from more serious deprivation, perhaps to replace an unemployed or sick breadwinner or to help a low-paid one. Indicator (g) represents the girls who leave school early in order to work, and (h), if read negatively to show the workers *without* any 'A' level qualifications, is an approximate measure of educational deprivation.[3]

Table 6.3. Correlation Matrix Between Indicators of Deprivation

	Unsk.	Unemp.	Sick	M.W. 30	No W.C.	1.5 PPR	S.W. 15-19	A levels
Unsk.	1.00							
Unemp.	0.705	1.00						
Sick	0.683	0.722	1.00					
M.W. 30	0.174	-0.009	0.153	1.00				
No W.C.	0.679	0.284	0.527	0.257	1.00			
1.5 PPR	0.569	0.589	0.445	0.221	-0.159	1.00		
S.W. 15-19	0.391	0.472	0.483	0.169	0.576	0.197	1.00	
A levels	-0.358	-0.119	-0.234	-0.064	-0.645	0.360	-0.685	1.00

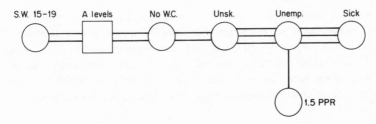

This matrix shows that all but one of our indicators of deprivation tend to concentrate in the same towns. If the correlations between them had been negative — or positive in the case of 'A' Level qualifications — that would show that hardships in the fields of employment, housing, health and education arise from different causes and affect different kinds of places; but in fact these deprivations are strongly associated, probably have common causes among which unemployment appears to play a central part, and tend to be concentrated in the same towns. But there may also be various influences affecting the distribution of unemployment — it could mean different things in different places.

(4) High status, vulnerability and deprivation

Finally we ask how these three patterns are related to each other. We bring the main evidence together in the next two tables.

Table 6.4. Correlation Matrix between Indicators of High Status and of Deprivation

	Professional	Degree	More than one car	Exclusive amenities
Unsk.	-0.763	-0.632	-0.756	-0.510
Unemp.	-0.546	-0.409	-0.641	-0.250
Sick	-0.570	-0.469	-0.623	-0.429
M.W. 30	-0.237	-0.286	-0.261	-0.468
No W.C.	-0.651	-0.583	-0.554	-0.700
1.5 PPR	-0.250	-0.155	-0.463	-0.160
S.W. 15-19	-0.849	-0.800	-0.722	-0.297
A levels	0.652	0.773	0.471	0.260

Only two of these variables will by definition have a negative relationship with each other (the number of households living in houses without an unshared inside W.C., and the number of households with exclusive use of all amenities). Nevertheless, all the indicators of deprivation are negatively related to all indicators of status. We have already shown that all but one of our indicators of deprivation tend to concentrate in the same towns. We now know that these are different towns. High status and deprivation are not concentrated in the same places.

Table 6.5. Correlation Matrix between Indicators of Vulnerability and Deprivation

	Unsk.	2A 5dep.	1A 2dep.	N.C.Born	15-24	45-64	65+
Unsk.	1.00	0.617	0.572	-0.206	0.536	-0.129	-0.139
Unemp.	0.705	0.668	0.603	-0.311	0.398	-0.153	0.009
Sick	0.683	0.525	0.498	0.295	0.221	0.067	0.065
M.W. 30	0.174	0.151	0.287	0.572	0.249	0.086	-0.141
No W.C.	0.679	0.298	0.346	-0.045	0.184	0.049	-0.040
1.5 PPR	0.569	0.565	0.434	0.083	0.394	-0.058	-0.129
S.W. 15-29	0.391	0.569	0.385	-0.122	0.301	-0.260	-0.214
A levels	-0.385	-0.252	-0.217	0.030	-0.020	0.061	-0.008

Table 6.5, showing the relationship between vulnerability and deprivation, presents a more complicated picture. The presence of the unskilled, the large families and the one-parent families in the first three columns of the table is related almost as positively to the indicators of deprivation as the high status distributions in the previous table were negatively related to the same indicators. The young age group represented in column 5 assumes a similar pattern, which is not surprising: where there are large families there are likely to be lots of young people. These are typical characteristics of the impoverished working class neighbourhood. Towns where such neighbourhoods predominate are still those most afflicted by many other kinds of deprivation. High status people who have greater choice about where they live go elsewhere.

Social Structure

In conclusion we summarise the main things which distinguish the towns to be compared in the next chapter where we use the rest of the 40 variables on which our analysis is based. Of the characteristics we have chosen to examine, the occupational structure represented by our five socio-economic groupings, ranging from the unskilled to the professional workers, goes further than anything else to explain other features of these towns. Others have reached similar conclusions before.[4]

Towns with a high proportion of non-manual workers tend also to have low proportions of all the more vulnerable groups, except old age pensioners. They have fewer people under 25 and fewer large families, one-parent families and sick people. These towns also tend to have a high concentration of service industries and government employment and fewer workers in manufacturing and mining, which is to be expected because service industries employ a large proportion of non-manual workers. They also have characteristics associated with high income and status such as advanced education, good housing, low unemployment, high car ownership and self-employment. Their higher reliance on travel to work by car suggests that many of these towns are some distance from the main centres of work, and their residents traverse a larger labour market area. They live in these more prosperous towns, but they may work elsewhere.

However the occupations which distinguish towns do not simply provide a contrast between towns for manual and non-manual workers. There are sex differences too. There is a marked absence of women workers in both the professional and the skilled manual groups: women are more highly concentrated in the intermediate and junior non-manual, and the semi-skilled manual groups — the lower halves of manual and of non-manual work. Thus towns with high concentrations of junior non-manual and semi-skilled manual workers have a lot of women at work, and are also the places where there are many married women with young children working. These towns also have relatively large numbers of citizens from the New Commonwealth.

Class contrasts between towns tend to follow two distinct polarisations. One separates the 'top' and 'bottom' of the social structure, distinguishing towns with a large proportion of professional and managerial workers and small proportions of semi-skilled and unskilled manual workers from towns with the opposite characteristics. The other separates the middle grades of the structure, distinguishing towns with a large proportion of the junior non-manual workers and a small proportion of skilled manual workers from towns with the opposite characteristics. It is the first of these two distinctions which tends to identify towns with the highest and lowest concentrations of deprivation and of vulnerable people (other than pensioners and those born in the New Commonwealth). The skilled working class tend to live in quite different environments from the unskilled, in places without the extremes of affluence and deprivation.

Housing

While the labour market, through the occupational structure, has a dominant influence on conditions in the towns in our study, the housing market plays an important secondary part by giving different kinds of people access to housing in different tenures — owner-occupied, privately rented or council owned. The occupational structure itself goes far to determine the tenure of housing. But tenure is not just the passive outcome of occupation. The form of available housing will exert some influence on the kinds of labour available in a town. Skilled manual workers hold a large share of council housing; they are probably attracted and retained in towns with plenty of council houses; and electorates in which skilled workers play a dominant part probably elect councils which build a lot of houses. We cannot be sure which are the dominant causal influences.

Owner-occupied housing is most heavily concentrated in areas which are predominantly non-manual and have high concentrations of professional and managerial workers. This may partly explain the low proportions of large families, one-parent families and sick people in such towns. Their main dependent group is the pensioners. Educational attainment is high, many households have more than one car, but relatively few women go to work — possibly because journeys to work are long, many women have childen to care for, and most families do not have more than one car. Families, to judge from their age and structure, tend to be smaller and children tend to leave home at an earlier age than elsewhere — probably to go on to further education.

Privately rented furnished and unfurnished housing cater for more varied and more transient groups. Towns with high proportions of this property have large numbers of single non-pensioner households, people born in the New Commonwealth and people in the 15-24 age group and the age groups over 45 — the young and the old. There is a large amount of sharing and many poorly equipped houses. Furnished housing tends to be overcrowded, the unfurnished to be ill-equipped. Furnished housing tends to be most common in prosperous towns where educational attainment is high, unemployment is low, high proportions of households own more than one car and female activity rates are high. Unfurnished housing is concentrated in towns with some of the opposite characteristics — high unemployment and few households with more than one car. But female activity rates tend to be high in these towns too.

Privately rented housing is usually old: most of it was built before the First World War. Thus it tends to stand close to the centres of towns, within easy reach of jobs — particularly in the service industries, public buildings and offices where a lot of women work. Women on their own, and households with several earners and no children tend to value access to the labour market and city centres more highly, and spacious dwellings and gardens less highly, than families with children.[5] That is why towns with a lot of high-density, privately rented housing will attract a lot of working women. Furnished rented housing particularly serves well educated young people who leave their parents' owner-occupied housing early but marry late. Unfurnished rented housing serves a much more heterogenous group, including some of the most deprived people. But we should beware of generalising: the role of privately rented housing varies from place to place.

Councils have succeeded in housing many of the more vulnerable groups to whom they have given priority: manual workers in general, large families and one-parent families, and the sick. The tendency to allocate council housing to large families produces considerable over-crowding in this sector of the market, but its houses are as well equipped with basic amenities as owner-occupied housing. The tenants' main problems probably lie in the labour market, as shown by the high concentrations of unemployment and the low female activity rates in towns with many council houses. Their dependence on bus transport suggests that council tenants have either a central location — in which case central areas are not offering enough jobs of the sort which these people can do — or a suburban location with poor transport services which confine them to too small a labour market. It may also be that this reasonably good and modestly priced housing, coupled with the difficulty of arranging exchanges between council tenants, has tied people to areas where employment prospects are poor.

Here we bring our analysis of city characteristics to a close. In the next chapter we give a picture of different kinds of cities viewed 'in the round'.

7 Different Kinds of Towns

In the last chapter we showed how the different characteristics of towns are related to each other. We now turn to consider each of our thirteen clusters of towns grouped together, by methods explained in Appendix II, on the basis of the 40 variables analysed in the previous chapter. These variables are listed in Appendix III. Here we describe and contrast the clusters, showing where each fits into the history of Britain's urban development — for similar towns generally have similar histories. Then, in the next chapter, we compare the experience of different kinds of people rather than the character of different kinds of towns.

The Clusters

The 154 towns we studied are listed in their clusters in Appendix I. These clusters are mapped and briefly described in the pages which follow. Our account of them is based on data for the year 1971. (Since then, some things will have changed.) For each cluster we have devised a name, but these names are merely our attempt to characterise them in a word or two. We also give, for each, the two towns which are, statistically speaking, most typical of the cluster. For those familiar with these places, their names will provide a more accurate description of the clusters.

Cluster 1 London: London and Cambridge

There are only two cities in this cluster and its scores are swamped by those of the capital which is much the largest of the two. Although London is rapidly declining in population, it has most of the labour market characteristics of expanding high status areas, and very little in common with the other inner conurbations. That is partly because London has been defined to include the whole Greater London area, including some of the city's more affluent suburbs. The other conurbation towns — places like Sheffield and Manchester — are defined as the

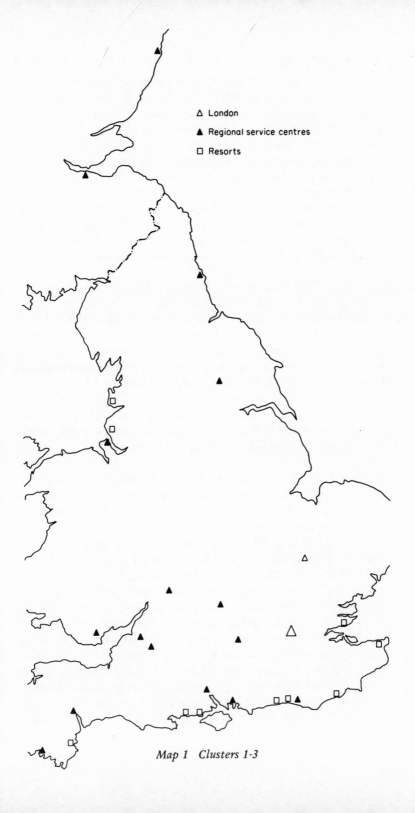

Map 1 Clusters 1-3

old county boroughs covering only the core of their urban area.

The junior non-manual occupations are heavily represented in these two towns, and skilled manual workers under-represented. That arises from their industrial structure which shows a high proportion of service industries and government employment, and a low proportion of manufacturing and mining. The dominance of the service sector explains the high female activity rates and the low rates of unemployment. The most distinctive features of this cluster, however, are its housing and demographic variables (the 'London dimension' illustrated in Figure 6.1, page 75). There is a very high proportion of furnished and shared accommodation, and an above average proportion of single non-pensioner households and people born in the New Commonwealth.

Cluster 2   Regional Service Centres: Bristol and Cardiff

Although the 16 cities in this cluster form an intuitively plausible category, they have relatively few distinctive features. They depend heavily on service industries and have a large proportion of non-manual workers. Unemployment is close to the national average but female activity rates are below average. The age groups over 45 are over-represented; so is owner-occupied and furnished rented housing.

These towns have relatively few New Commonwealth immigrants or other vulnerable groups. The marginal, or least typical, city falling into this cluster was Oxford which in some of our preliminary analyses was grouped with London, Cambridge and Edinburgh.

Cluster 3   Resorts: Bournemouth and Thanet

The 10 Resorts form a very stable and distinctive group of cities: a cluster of this sort was found in nearly every one of the ten cluster analyses we carried out. They have a very high proportion of professional and managerial workers and a very low proportion of unskilled manual workers. Their most distinctive characteristic, however, is their high proportion of self-employed people, many of whom must be working in tourist trades. Their industrial structure depends heavily on service industries. Despite this, female activity rates are low, which may be because of the large proportion of higher socio-economic groups, amongst whom few women go to work. Unemployment is slightly above average, and that may be because the tourist trades experience heavy seasonal fluctuations. These towns have high proportions of people in all the age groups above 45. It is possible that some of these, though registered as unemployed, are in effect retiring early. There are few large families in this cluster, which is not surprising in view of their high proportion of older people. Housing in the Resorts is predominantly owner-occupied or privately rented, and there is little council housing; but the quality of their housing is generally good, and the large proportion of elderly small households produces a substantial amount of low occupancy. In these towns there are few indicators of deprivation other than unemployment, and few vulnerable groups other than the old.

Cluster 4 Residential Suburbs: Chertsey and Walton-on-Thames, and Solihull

The 10 Residential Suburbs are growing faster than any other cluster except the New Towns. They have the highest proportions of professional and managerial workers and a marked absence of all the manual groups. Their industrial structure depends heavily on service industries, and unemployment is low. Female activity rates, however, are low too. Many of those at work must commute to jobs elsewhere.

These towns show all the indicators of high status and very little of deprivation. Educational attainment and the proportion of households with more than one car are high, and many people travel to work by car. Houses in most cases have all the standard amenities and low densities of occupation, and they are mainly owner-occupied. These towns have few vulnerable groups such as one-parent families, large families or people born in the New Commonwealth, and they have large proportions in the prime age groups between 25 and 44 years old.

These first four clusters contain the major service oriented towns of Britain. The remaining clusters all depend more heavily upon manufacturing. Some of the service towns, like London, are geared to national and international markets, some like the Regional Service Centres, to regional markets, some, like the Residential Suburbs, to more local markets, and some, like the Resorts, are specifically organised for tourism. But they all share certain characteristics. They have high proportions of white collar workers, few vulnerable groups and little deprivation. They have a lot of privately owned housing – particularly privately rented housing. And most of them are in the southern half of England.

Cluster 5 New Industrial Suburbs: Pudsey and Worcester

The main difference between the Residential Suburbs and the New Industrial Suburbs lies in their industrial structures. The New Industrial

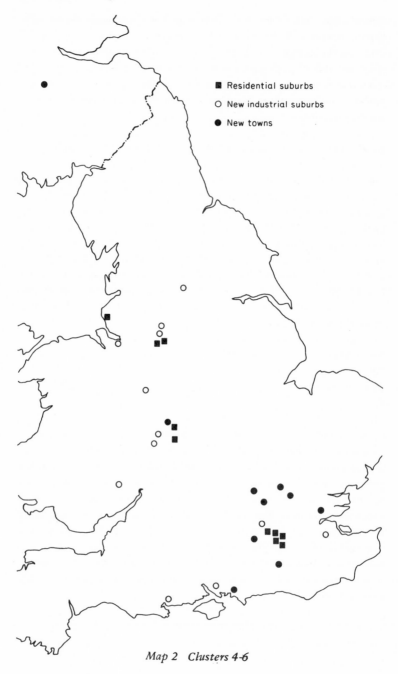

Map 2 Clusters 4-6

Suburbs also have a smaller proportion of the professional and managerial groups and are not as affluent as the Residential Suburbs.

It is difficult to give a collective name to the 12 towns in this cluster. They are the slowest growing of the family of rapidly growing urban areas. Despite having a large proportion of professional and managerial workers and few unskilled manual workers, they depend fairly heavily on manufacturing. Unemployment is below average. The occupational structure of manufacturing industry in these towns differs somewhat from other areas: elsewhere, manufacturing tends to be correlated with a low proportion of professional and managerial workers and high unemployment. It may also be that many of the professional workers in these towns commute to work elsewhere — an explanation which gains support from the unusually large numbers who travel to work by car, and from the proximity of some of these towns to large conurbations. The New Industrial Suburbs have high proportions of owner-occupiers and households owning more than one car, and high proportions of well-equipped houses, large houses and houses with low densities of occupation.

These towns lack most indicators of deprivation. They have high proportions in the 'prime' age group between 25 and 44, and few in the vulnerable groups such as one-parent families, large families, the New Commonwealth born and the 15-24 age group.

Cluster 6 The New Towns: Hertford and Stevenage, and East Kilbride

The 10 New Towns are the fastest growing cluster. Each has a new town in it, but most also have older urban areas too. They show a number of exceptions to general trends which point to the effects of planned interventions in the market. They depend heavily on manufacturing, yet they have almost as many non-manual workers, and especially professional and managerial workers, as the Residential and New Industrial Suburbs. They are more self-contained than these suburbs; thus, despite their heavy use of cars for travel to work, more of their non-manual workers must actually be working in these towns. They also have a type of manufacturing which is very different in occupational structure from the older manufacturing industries of other towns. They have very low unemployment and high female activity rates which are both unusual for manufacturing towns. The New Towns' other unusual feature is that despite high proportions of non-manual workers, a large proportion of their housing belongs to the local authorities. This housing is also of much better standard than in most areas dominated by council housing, both in its amenities (in which local authority housing is normally good) and in densities of occupation (for which local authority housing tends to be bad).

There are few of the vulnerable groups in the New Towns: all indicators of deprivation are low and high status indicators are common. They have high proportions of people in the prime age group of 25-44 and many children under 14. All six of the clusters so far listed are distinguished by having higher proportions of non-manual workers than the remaining seven. They have less deprivation, more high status groups and fewer vulnerable groups than other clusters. The populations of the last three of them are the fastest growing of all clusters. (Our indicator of growth is the rate of change in the size of the electorate — the population aged 18 and over — between 1955 and 1970.)

Cluster 7   Welsh Mining Towns: Rhondda and Aberdare

The three Welsh Mining Towns are at the other end of the growth spectrum, delining in population faster than any other cluster. They have a very large proportion of skilled manual workers and above average proportions of other manual workers, but few non-manual workers. That arises from their industrial structure which depends heavily on coal mining and manufacturing. Unemployment is high and female activity rates low. One of the most distinctive features of these towns is the very high proportion of workers who are sick. This presumably arises partly from their age structure, which includes high proportions of those aged 45-64, and partly from conditions in the mines. But other factors may also be at work: sickness is more common in many other parts of Wales too, and in occupations such as the civil service not specially exposed to hazards to health. It may be more acceptable in Wales than it is elsewhere to describe yourself as "sick". The quality of the housing stock may affect people's health: housing in these towns is primarily owner-occupied and (as a result of long periods of out-migration) it is used at low densities; but many of these houses are old. This cluster of towns has the highest proportion of houses without the exclusive use of all amenities. Educational attainment in the Mining Towns is below average. That may be due partly to the large numbers of more highly qualified people who leave them to find work elsewhere. In Wales as a whole educational attainment bears the marks of deep social divisons. The proportions of school leavers who do well and go on to full-time higher education are above the national average, but the proportion who leave without any qualifications at all is larger than in any other region of England and Wales.[1]

Although the Welsh Mining Towns show many signs of deprivation

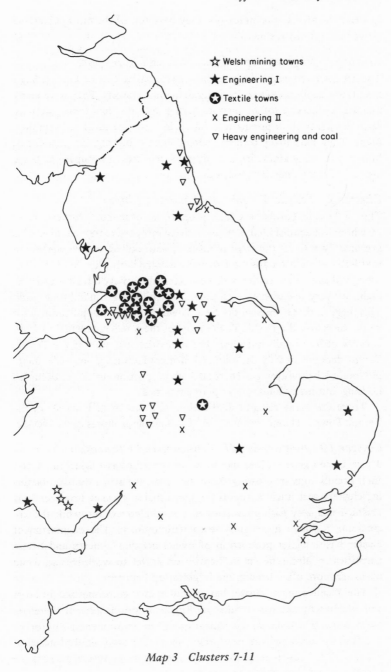

Map 3   Clusters 7-11

and lack the high status indicators, they have few of the most vulnerable groups except old age pensioners.

Cluster 8   Engineering I: Doncaster and Stockport

The 19 towns to which we gave the uninformative title of Engineering I have fewer distinctive characteristics than most clusters. They have many manual workers, a lot of manufacturing industry, low female activity rates, low growth in population, but below average rates of unemployment. They have many owner-occupied houses, but high proportions of houses with poor amenities and with low densities of occupation. There are few of the vulnerable groups in these towns.

Cluster 9   Textile Towns: Bolton and Oldham

The 16 Textile Towns have high proportions of manual workers, many of whom are semi-skilled. Female activity rates are extremely high: this presumably reflects the large number of semi-skilled women workers in textiles. In no cluster are there so many women with pre-school children doing full-time jobs. In the New Towns female activity rates are nearly as high, but very few women with pre-school children are in full-time work. This suggests that women in the New Towns have good opportunities for work whereas in the Textile Towns more of them feel compelled to work because of low family incomes. The industrial structure of the Textile Towns depends heavily on mining and manufacturing, but male unemployment is below average. There are high proportions of owner-occupied housing, but many houses have poor amenities.

There are many signs of deprivation, and few of high status, in the Textile Towns. Their concentration of vulnerable groups is above average.

Cluster 10   Engineering II: Swindon and Gloucester

These 14 towns are rather like those we described as Engineering I, but their populations are growing. Both, however, are primarily manufacturing clusters with their residents doing manual work. The Engineering II cluster has a very high proportion of semi-skilled workers while the Engineering I cluster has slightly less unemployment. The Engineering II cluster has a higher proportion of owner-occupied houses and better amenities. It also relies more heavily on travel to work by car, while buses are more often used in the Engineering I cluster.

The Engineering II cluster has an above average proportion of large and one-parent families (unlike the Engineering I cluster). It therefore has a larger than average concentration of the more vulnerable groups, but slightly fewer indicators of deprivation than that would lead us to expect. These towns are particularly interesting for several reasons. In Chapter 10 we discuss them in greater detail.

Cluster 11   Heavy Engineering and Coal: Walsall and Farnworth

This cluster of 22 towns is also growing. They have high proportions of manual workers, particularly the more skilled, and very low proportions of intermediate and junior non-manual workers. These are fairly prosperous manufacturing cities — masculine and working class. Female activity rates are extremely low and unemployment is below average. They have high proportions of council houses and above average proportions of houses without the basic amenities. Their formal educational attainments are particularly poor, which may be due in part to the large numbers of youngsters who leave school early for apprenticeships.

These towns do not have severe concentrations of deprivation, and they do not have large numbers of the vulnerable groups.

Cluster 12   The Inner Conurbations; Nottingham and Manchester

The 14 towns of the Inner Conurbations cluster are declining fairly rapidly in population. They have high proportions of manual workers and especially high concentrations of semi-skilled and unskilled workers. This, coupled with their dependence on manufacturing industries, differentiates them from London which depends more heavily on non-manual work in service industries. The Inner Conurbations have, after Central Scotland, the highest proportion of unemployed men. Female activity rates are slightly above average. They also have above average concentrations of council housing, and a large number of houses lacking the basic amenities. The density of occupation, however, is fairly low and, unlike London, they have few shared dwellings. Educational attainment among the working population is particulaly low and many people are sick. For travel to work they rely heavily on buses.

The Inner Conurbations have a high proportion of some vulnerable groups such as one-parent families and large families but no more than average numbers of people born in the New Commonwealth. They have relatively few old people and few people in the prime age groups, but they have large numbers of children under 15 and of the unemployment-prone 15-24 age group. In all, they have one of the highest proportions of the vulnerable groups and many signs of deprivation. We discuss these towns in greater detail in Chapter 9.

Cluster 13   Central Scotland: Glasgow and Paisley

These six towns show more signs than any other cluster of nearly every kind of deprivation. That is partly because the cluster's scores are

Map 4   Clusters 12-13

heavily affected by conditions in Glasgow, which is by far the largest of them. The cluster is declining in population. It depends heavily on manufacturing and mining industries, and has a very high proportion of unskilled workers and a very low proportion of professional and managerial workers. Unemployment is higher than in any other cluster. The general female activity rates are near the average, but an unusually large proportion of mothers with pre-school children work full-time. Central Scotland has by far the highest proportion of council housing and below average proportions of all other housing tenures. The proportion of workers recorded in the Census as having 'A' level qualifications is above average, but that is probably due to Scotland's examination system which enables pupils to take 'Scottish Highers', a different examination, in a considerable number of subjects a year earlier than the usual age for 'A' level candidates. The proportion of workers with a degree is below average. These towns depend heavily upon buses for travel to work, just as the Inner Conurbations do.

This cluster has very high concentrations of vulnerable groups such as one-parent and large families and the age groups under 25: it is clearly the most deprived and the most vulnerable of all the clusters. We discuss it again in Chapter 9.

This verbal summary of a massive quantity of figures and the maps attached to it give only a rough and ready account of the characteristics of these towns. Readers who want to take the analysis of the clusters further will find more information in the Appendices. Here we try to give a more precise answer to the general question: How much do these clusters differ? That question may be approached by first asking which clusters most resemble each other?

There is no natural point at which to stop the grouping together of towns — no uniquely authoritative set of urban categories. The process could have been halted anywhere from our starting point of 154 individual towns to the point at which all 154 are combined into the one category of British towns, which are themselves only a small subset of the world's towns. The two clusters which most closely resemble each other in respect of the variables chosen for our analysis are those whose combination would lose the smallest amount of difference, or variance, in our data. We can combine successive clusters, following this rule so as to minimise at each stage the loss of variance between the groups which remain. This process is portrayed in Figure 7.1, which is called a dendogram. Reading from left to right, it shows the order in which our 13 clusters would be combined and (in figures along the margin of the dendogram) the variance lost at each stage. Only 3 per cent of the variance would have been lost if we had converted these 13 clusters into seven 'families' by combining the most similar ones up to the point shown by a dotted line drawn across the dendogram scale at 3.00. The clusters of towns listed in Appendix I are grouped in these families as a way of showing the main similarities and differences between them.

It may be more revealing to consider the process of subdivision into clusters from the opposite point of view — from the right hand side of the dendogram — because this shows in the order of their importance the biggest differences between the main types of British towns. The cluster analysis distinguishes two major groups of towns — the first six and the remaining seven. At the junctions in this dendogram we have shown the one characteristic which most sharply distinguishes the groups being divided. The variable which most clearly distinguishes between the two main groups of clusters is the proportion of intermediate and junior non-manual workers in these towns. The first six clusters are white collar towns (and particularly lower middle class towns) with large proportions of these workers. The other seven clusters are broadly working class towns with low proportions of workers in the more routine non-manual jobs.

The next junction in the dendogram divides the first six clusters into two groups of three, distinguishing the New Industrial and Residential Suburbs and the New Towns from the remainder, particularly because they are growing in population.

Next Central Scotland divides from the other six predominantly working class towns in the bottom half of the dendogram. The extent of overcrowding is the variable which most clearly distinguishes these Scottish Towns from the rest. Then the Resorts divide from London and the Regional Service Centres; the large proportion of old people in the Resorts distinguishes this cluster from the other two. Then the Inner Conurbations divide from the Welsh Mining, Engineering and Textile clusters: their large proportion of privately rented unfurnished houses being their most distinctive characteristic. Finally the Regional Service Centres divide from London; London's high proportion of immigrants born in the New Commonwealth is the characteristic which most clearly distinguishes it from the rest. The subdivisions made so far leave us with seven families of towns. Two of these families, in the centre of the scale, contain several clusters, but these towns are more like each other than are those we have already distinguished.

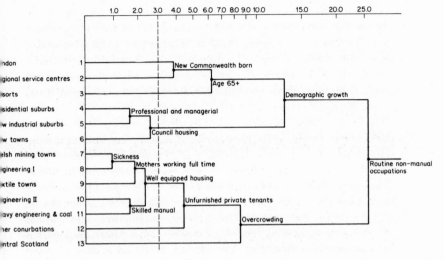

Figure 7.1

This analysis shows that British cities can be divided into two major groups: the industrial, working class towns, mainly in the North, depending heavily on manufacturing (see Maps 3 and 4); and the more prosperous white collar towns, mainly in the South, depending heavily on private service industries and government (see Maps 1 and 2). They might be described as 'traditional Britain' and 'new Britain'; the first industrial revolution, and the second. These tags capture some of their essential differences.

Within 'traditional Britain' two clusters distinguish themselves from a large group of five manufacturing, mining and textile towns: the deprived, heavily industrial towns of Central Scotland, and the central cores of the great conurbations (see Map 4). We discuss them in greater detail in Chapter 9.

'New Britain' consists, roughly speaking, of four groups of towns: (i) the three most rapidly growing and prosperous, mainly suburban and southern (see Map 2); (ii) the coastal Resorts full of retired people and service trades; (iii) the capital; and (iv) the Regional Service Centres — 'mini-capitals' — (all shown on Map 1).

Changes and Achievements
We said at the beginning of Chapter 6 that there have been three main trends in British urban development during this century. The first is the southward movement of economic activity which has drained much

of the industrial prosperity from the older industrial centres built up during the nineteenth century in the North and in peripheral parts of the country. The second is the decentralisation of the largest conurbations. The third is the growth of tourism and retirement centres along the coasts. The clusters are in effect a map of these historical trends. They show a polarisation along geographical, industrial and class lines.

Among the first six 'new Britain' clusters, 62 per cent of the towns are in the South West, the South East or East Anglia. If the East and West Midlands and Wales are added to these three regions, they account for 73 per cent of the towns in the 'new' clusters. All these depend heavily on work in the non-manual occupations. Except for the modern manufacturing developed in the New Towns and New Industrial Suburbs, they all depend heavily upon the service sector of the economy. Among the remaining clusters representing 'traditional Britain', 70 per cent of the towns are in the three Northern Regions or in Scotland. They depend heavily on manufacturing and mining, and on manual work.

Superimposed upon this North–South pattern is the decentralisation of the conurbations. Whereas the former movement of economic activity is based upon differences between manufacturing and services and between manual and non-manual work, the latter reflects to a much greater extent the distinctions between unskilled manual work and the most skilled professional and managerial work. Both kinds of worker may actually work in the same conurbation centres, but our data, derived from the Census, shows where people live. The resident populations of these clusters are more sharply polarised than their working populations.

The Resorts are in many respects a subdivision of the group of clusters on the fringes of the great conurbations. Like the Suburbs and New Towns, they have growing populations, many white collar workers and a considerable number of commuters who travel to bigger cities each day to work. But they have characteristics of their own too – a lot of older people, many self-employed workers and fairly heavy unemployment.

Tables 7.1 and 7.2 rank the clusters according to the incidence in each of indicators of high status and of deprivation. The Residential Suburbs, the New Towns and the New Industrial Suburbs (mainly in the South) consistently appear at the 'best' end of these rank orders – at the top of the status rankings in Table 7.1 and at the bottom of the deprivation rankings in Table 7.2. Central Scotland, the Inner Conurbations (mainly in the North) and the Welsh Mining Towns consistently appear at the 'worst' end, with the fewest high status indicators and most signs of deprivation.

Table 10.1, on page 135, ranks clusters in the same way according to the presence of potentially vulnerable people – the unskilled, large families, one-parent families, the youngest workers, old people and people born in the New Commonwealth. The rank orders take the patterns already described in Chapter 6. The most frequent victims of working class poverty — the unskilled, the largest families, lone parents and the youngest workers — are concentrated in the towns of old, industrial Britain, most notably Central Scotland and the Inner Conurbations. The distributions of older people and those born in the New Commonwealth take different patterns.

The principal patterns of affluence and deprivation to be seen among the cities of Britain are the imprint, at urban scale, of national trends in the economy. Within these extremes the rankings are less clearly related to these major trends. If we are looking for evidence that planned intervention at the urban scale can significantly improve or redistribute the general pattern of opportunities which cities offer their people, it may be among the clusters lying within these extremes that we shall find it. Moreover the impact achieved may only be a fairly modest one. Individual cities can be transformed by concentrating new, footloose industry in them; the New Towns are the proof of this. But their prosperity may be achieved at the cost of impoverishing other places which might otherwise have benefited from the same investment of human talent and capital: they will only have made a contribution to the national economy if they helped to generate innovation and development which would not otherwise have occurred. Individual sectors of the urban economy can be transformed too; the rehousing in good homes of hundreds of thousands of families from the slums of many cities proves this. The deviation of the best and worst housed clusters from the average (shown in column 3 of Table 7.1) is much smaller than the differences in their social class composition, their educational attainment or their car ownership (shown in the other columns of this table). But the opportunities of council tenants in other sectors of the economy — for work, earnings and education, for example — may not have been greatly affected by that achievement. We will explore these difficult questions in later chapters.

Table 7.1. Rankings of Clusters by Indicators of High Status

Professional and managerial workers		Households owning a car		Houses with all standard amenities		Workers with a degree	
Residential Suburbs	213	Residential Suburbs	269	New Towns	119	Residential Suburbs	204
Resorts	139	New Towns	179	Residential Suburbs	117	New Towns	128
New Towns	138	New Industrial Suburbs	159	New Industrial Suburbs	111	New Industrial Suburbs	128
New Industrial Suburbs	131	London	114	Resorts	107	Regional Service Centres	117
London	119	Resorts	108	Engineering II	106	London	115
Regional Service Centres	102	Engineering II	102	Heavy Engineering and Coal	102	Resorts	108
Engineering II	85	Regional Service Centres	97	Regional Service Centres	101	Engineering I	94
Engineering I	85	Engineering I	83	Central Scotland	101	Engineering II	86
Textile Towns	81	Heavy Engineering and Coal	78	Engineering I	99	Central Scotland	80
Heavy Engineering and Coal	72	Textile Towns	71	London	96	Textile Towns	79
Inner Conurbations	70	Inner Conurbations	62	Inner Conurbations	95	Inner Conurbations	73
Central Scotland	63	Welsh Mining Towns	51	Textile Towns	93	Welsh Mining Towns	72
Welsh Mining Towns	53	Central Scotland	40	Welsh Mining Towns	69	Heavy Engineering and Coal	69

A score of 100 is the average score for all people or households in the 154 towns in the cluster analysis.

Table 7.2. Rankings of Clusters by Indicators of Deprivation

Unskilled		Unemployed		Sick		Houses without unshared indoor WC		Overcrowding (>1.5 PPR)		Economically active women aged 15-20		Workers with 'A' Levels	
Central Scotland	154	Central Scotland	205	Welsh Mining Towns	280	Welsh Mining Towns	333	Central Scotland	487	Heavy engineering and coal	113	Welsh Mining Towns	62
Inner con-urbations	130	Inner con-urbations	147	Central Scotland	188	Textile towns	179	London	117	Central Scotland	109	Heavy engineering and coal	63
Textile towns	115	Welsh Mining Towns	122	Inner con-urbations	138	Inner con-urbations	154	Inner con-urbations	97	Inner con-urbations	107	Inner con-urbations	69
Welsh Mining Towns	113	Resorts	106	Textile towns	113	Engineering I	144	Regional service centres	83	Textile towns	105	Textile towns	72
Heavy engineering and coal	107	Engineering II	100	Heavy engineering and coal	111	Heavy engineering and coal	131	Textile towns	75	Engineering II	104	Engineering I	81
Engineering I	104	Regional service centres	100	Engineering I	107	Engineering II	92	Engineering II	69	Engineering I	104	Engineering II	83
Engineering II	101	Heavy engineering and coal	94	Resorts	97	Regional service centres	73	Heavy engineering and coal	68	Welsh Mining Towns	102	Resorts	97
Regional service centres	101	Textile towns	93	Engineering I	91	London	68	New towns	46	London	94	New industrial suburbs	109
London	88	Engineering I	89	Regional service centres	84	Central Scotland	67	Engineering I	45	Regional service centres	94	London	121
New industrial suburbs	70	London	76	Engineering II	74	New industrial suburbs	65	Resorts	40	New industrial suburbs	93	Regional service centres	124
Resorts	60	New industrial suburbs	63	London	70	Resorts	35	Welsh Mining Towns	33	Resorts	92	New towns	124
New towns	56	New towns	57	New industrial suburbs	60	Residential suburbs	31	New industrial suburbs	32	New towns	92	Central Scotland	145
Residential suburbs	35	Residential suburbs	49	Residential suburbs	41	New towns	25	Residential suburbs	23	Residential suburbs	76	Residential suburbs	167

8 From Towns to People

Thus far we have asked which kinds of cities are in various crude senses doing best and worst. Next we must ask where particular kinds of people do best and worst. The main evidence we have which shows the conditions experienced by different kinds of people (rather than the conditions in different kinds of towns) deals with employment and unemployment, car ownership, travel to work and educational attainment among each of the five categories into which we have grouped the larger numbers of socio-economic groups used by the Registrar General.[1]

Some of this evidence is summarised for the population of our 154 towns in Tables 8.1-8.4. Not surprisingly, the upper occupational groups are more likely than the lower to own cars, to drive to work in them and to have formal academic qualifications, and they are less likely to be unemployed.

Prosperity and Equality

Do these different grades of worker fare better or worse, in comparison with their own peers elsewhere, in particular kinds of town? Or do all gain and suffer equally from the affluence or poverty of each town? In order to explore that question the next tables show, for each cluster, the unemployment, car ownership and mode of travel to work of each occupational group, expressing the figure for each as a percentage of the weighted average for that group in all 154 towns — that is to say the average for all the people in these towns. (Thus a figure of 100 for unemployment among semi-skilled manual workers in a particular cluster would mean that semi-skilled workers in this cluster experience the average amount of unemployment for such workers in all towns. A score of 150 would mean they are 50 per cent more likely to be unemployed than semi-skilled workers in all towns. To make these tables easier to read we range the clusters from left to right, placing on the left the clusters which are most deprived in terms of whatever variable the table deals with and placing the most affluent on the right. (Where that

Table 8.1. *Occupational Groups by Industry: 1971*

	Mining and manufacturing	Services and central and local government	Other	Total
	%	%	%	%
Professional and managerial	26	60	14	100
Other non manual	21	69	10	100
Skilled manual	54	19	27	100
Semi-skilled manual	51	37	12	100
Unskilled manual	36	43	21	100
Total	38	46	16	100

Table 8.2. *Occupational Groups, Unemployment and Car Ownership: 1971*

	Unemployed (%)	Cars per household
Professional and managerial	2	0.99
Other non-manual	2	0.55
Skilled manual	4	0.54
Semi-skilled manual	5	0.32
Unskilled manual	10	0.18

Table 8.3. *Occupational Groups and Mode of Travel to Work: 1971*

	Car	Train	Bus	Pedal	Walk	Other	Total
	%	%	%	%	%	%	%
Professional and managerial	57	13	10	1	11	9	100
Other non-manual	30	13	33	3	18	4	100
Skilled manual	39	5	28	6	15	7	100
Semi-skilled manual	17	4	40	6	28	5	100
Unskilled manual	10	4	43	6	32	4	100
All workers	32	8	31	5	19	6	100

Table 8.4. *Occupational Groups and Highest Academic Qualifications Attained: 1971*

	'A' level	Degree
	%	%
Professional and managerial	28	28
Other non-manual	16	14
Skilled manual	4	1
Semi-skilled manual	3	*
Unskilled manual	1	*

*Less than 0.5%.

rank order varies for different occupational groups we have taken the figures for unskilled workers as the basis for our presentation.)

Table 8.5 shows that the clusters on the left with the highest rates of unemployment for the unskilled tend to have high scores for unemployment for all groups; likewise those on the right with low unemployment among the unskilled tend to have low scores for all groups. Thus all classes benefit from a city's prosperity and all suffer from its poverty.

But in the poorer clusters on the left of Table 8.5 unemployment is worse (in relation to their own class elsewhere) for the manual workers, and for the least skilled in particular, than it is for non-manual workers, and the professional and managerial workers in particular. Likewise in the more prosperous clusters on the right of the table, unemployment is lower for manual workers, and the least skilled in particular (in relation to their own class elsewhere) than it is for non-manual workers, and the professional and managerial workers in particular. For clusters in the middle, with rates of unemployment closer to the average, the scores for different social groups are similar. There are exceptions to this generalisation. The Resorts, for example, have a generally bad rate of unemployment which is particularly high for non-manual workers. That may be because they have a large proportion of older, semi-retired people in these groups who register for work without much chance of getting a regular job – but our evidence cannot verify that suggestion. London too is unusual in having an incidence of unemployment among the unskilled which is appreciably lower than the rates among higher status groupings would lead us to expect. So, although all classes suffer from unemployment in the less prosperous towns, the least skilled suffer most; and although all gain from the prosperity of more fortunate towns, the least skilled gain most.

This finding can be presented in another way by showing the range between the highest and the lowest cluster scores for unemployment in each social class, and also – to avoid the influence of freak values – the range between the (unweighted) average of the three highest and the three lowest scores. We do that in Table 8.6 which shows that the range between the best and the worst is much greater for manual workers, and for the unskilled in particular, than for non-manual workers, and the professional and managerial workers in particular.[2] Scores for skilled and semi-skilled manual workers follow much the same patterns.

These figures show that the more prosperous towns of 'new Britain' – the New Towns, London and the New Industrial and Residential Suburbs – tended in 1971 both to offer more opportunities for work to all social classes, and to offer a more equal distribution of these

Table 8.5. Percentage of Economically Active Males and Females Unemployed, by Occupational Groups in Each Cluster

	Central Scotland	Welsh Mining Towns	Inner Con- urbations	Resorts	Engineering II	Heavy Engineering and Coal	Textile Towns	Regional Service Centres	Engineering I	In- dustrial Suburbs	Resi- dential Suburbs	London	New Towns
Professional and managerial	157	145	118	158	95	87	94	108	105	93	64	92	75
Other non-manual	161	145	121	165	88	80	94	104	90	79	67	94	62
Skilled manual	210	163	132	109	88	95	92	96	92	63	53	81	52
Semi-skilled manual	209	152	130	118	94	96	102	106	85	61	64	69	52
Unskilled manual	228	169	133	108	97	96	96	90	89	64	60	55	48

*Table 8.6.   Range from Highest to Lowest Cluster Scores for
Unemployment in Table 8.5, by Occupational Groups[2]*

	Lowest score (a)	Highest score (b)	Range (b-a) (c)	Average of		Range (e-d) (f)
				3 lowest scores (d)	3 highest scores (e)	
Professional and managerial	64	158	94	77	153	76
Other non-manual	62	165	103	69	157	88
Skilled manual	52	210	158	56	168	112
Semi-skilled manual	52	209	157	59	164	105
Unskilled manual	48	228	180	54	177	123

opportunities than the less prosperous towns of 'traditional Britain' — Central Scotland, the Welsh Mining Towns and the Inner Conurbations. As the great majority of manual workers are concentrated in 'traditional Britain' while a much higher proportion of the white collar workers are concentrated in 'new Britain', that might suggest that the distribution of people among towns reinforces inequality between these classes. Renewed economic growth may, however, create more towns of the 'new Britain' type, making the country more prosperous and more equal. On the other hand, the withdrawal of labour and capital from 'traditional Britain' and its diversion to 'new Britain', which is necessary to make the country competitive, may also leave manual workers and the unskilled impoverished in the towns of 'traditional Britain'. If so, faster growth and greater prosperity could make half the towns of Britain more unequal. Thus we must know more before we can offer any confident forecasts or prescriptions.

Car ownership and travel to work by car are important indicators of status and of the geographical scale of the markets to which a household has access. Tables 8.7 and 8.8 show the number of cars per household and the number of workers travelling by car to work for different occupational groups, using the same indices as before. Again the clusters are arranged in rank order of scores for the unskilled from left to right — starting on the left with the clusters in which the unskilled are doing worst.

The message of each table is much the same as before. Manual workers in general, and the least skilled in particular, generally do best in the more prosperous towns of 'new Britain' — the New Towns, the Residential and New Industrial Suburbs and London. They do much worse in the 'traditional Britain' of Central Scotland, the Inner Conurbations

Table 8.7. *Cars per Household, by Occupational Group in Each Cluster*

	Central Scotland	Inner Con-urbations	Textile Towns	Welsh Mining Towns	Heavy Engineering and Coal	Engineering I	Regional Service Centres	Resorts	Engineering II	London	Residential Suburbs	Industrial Suburbs	New Towns
Professional and managerial	79	88	96	76	101	97	95	91	105	98	129	115	119
Other non-manual	65	82	95	85	111	101	99	95	118	93	153	131	146
Skilled manual	55	80	86	74	91	91	102	113	115	115	156	126	146
Semi-skilled manual	50	77	76	97	103	98	101	101	132	105	160	137	169
Unskilled	43	67	71	96	97	99	112	119	123	128	181	152	187
All occupational groups	58	75	84	76	93	95	101	105	111	106	173	133	151

Table 8.8. Travel to Work by Car, by Occupational Group in Each Cluster

	Central Scotland	Inner Con-urbations	Textile Towns	Heavy Engineering and Coal	London	Engineering I	Regional Service Centres	Engineering II	In-dustrial Suburbs	Resi-dential Suburbs	Resorts	Welsh Mining Towns	New Towns
Professional and managerial	96	99	108	114	80	114	105	112	122	117	96	99	116
Other non-manual	66	84	105	122	72	115	111	122	148	151	93	124	147
Skilled manual	62	84	85	96	101	97	111	116	125	146	121	91	144
Semi-skilled manual	62	76	77	107	85	102	109	138	143	154	128	138	173
Unskilled	46	64	72	98	103	104	119	127	161	165	163	192	200
All occupational groups	64	80	91	104	86	105	109	117	139	156	122	104	148

and the Textile Towns. The unskilled are more than four times as likely to own cars and to travel to work by car in the New Towns as they are in Central Scotland. The differences for non-manual workers, and for the professional and managerial workers in particular, run in a similar direction, but to a less striking degree. The 'top' group of professional and managerial workers are only about 50 per cent more likely to own cars in the New Towns (and 60 per cent more likely in Residential Suburbs) than they are in Central Scotland. That difference in the social 'gradients' of opportunities for the social classes in towns of different types may reflect the fact that car ownership and use is nearing a ceiling at which everyone will have one car and few have more than one. The figures, it might be argued, show how close each class is to that ceiling. But the argument is weak (more and more families own several cars) and the differences are in any case real. They show, once more, that the more prosperous city generally tends to be the more equal city. But once again it cannot be assumed that further growth will necessarily lead to greater equality. It could also have a regressive effect, leaving many of the less skilled increasingly impoverished in the less prosperous cities.

There are deviations from this pattern, but they are not surprising to those who know the places concerned. The Welsh Mining Towns (Cluster 7) are rather low on car ownership for all occupational groups, but high on travel to work by car — particularly for the less skilled workers many of whom, as pits have closed, share cars to get to work in the new industries growing up along the coastal plain between Swansea and Newport. London takes an opposite pattern, being higher on car ownership than on travel to work by car: the capital's high densities, parking problems and relatively good public transport probably explain that.

The distribution of academic qualifications shows a somewhat similar pattern. Qualifications are greater amongst all groups in 'new Britain' than in 'traditional Britain', and the differences tend to be greater for the less skilled than for workers in jobs of higher status. But the meaning of these figures is harder to interpret. It may be that the industries of 'traditional Britain' reward people who learn through apprenticeships rather by taking academic qualifications. Education is a topic to which we return in Chapter 11.

In an earlier chapter we picked on mothers with children under school age as a potentially vulnerable group, and suggested that, given the lack of nursery facilities, those who work full-time at this stage may be doing so reluctantly in order to keep the family out of poverty, while those who work for fewer than eight hours a week are more likely to have chosen willingly to do so. Alternatively, we might avoid speculation about motives and simply note that mothers in many parts of the country have constantly demanded more pàrt-time work, and ask which towns have been most successful in giving them what they want. Table 8.9 contrasts this aspect of the clusters, presenting them in numerical order.

The general pattern of women's employment in these towns will depend on the local industrial structure. There will be more work for women in the Textile Towns and less in the Welsh Mining Towns, for example. But if our hypotheses are correct, then clusters which have abnormally small numbers of mothers with pre-school children working full-time and abnormally large numbers working for less than eight hours a week can be thought of as being 'kinder' to this potentially vulnerable group of families than those with the opposite pattern. The table shows that the Residential and New Industrial Suburbs, and the New Towns — all typical of 'new Britain' — are in this sense kinder places than Central Scotland, the Welsh Mining Towns and the Textile Towns — all typical of 'traditional Britain'. Roughly speaking, a mother with a child under school age would be half as likely to work full-time and twice as likely to work for less than eight hours a week in the New Towns as she would be in Central Scotland.

Immigrants

To conclude this chapter we show in Table 8.10 how immigrants are distributed among towns of different kinds, growing at varying rates. The clusters are again ranked in numerical order.

The table shows that London, despite its low ranking in growth (its electorate is actually declining) attracts immigrants from all parts of the world. Only for those born in Pakistan does it have fractionally less than the average proportion found in all towns.

The Irish are most concentrated in the Inner Conurbations and Engineering II clusters — in that order. Those from the Old Commonwealth go to Residential Suburbs, Resorts and New Towns. Africans, Indians and (particularly) Pakistanis go to Textile Towns, and the Pakistanis also go to the Inner Conurbations. Those born in Hong Kong, China, Malaya and other oriental countries go to Regional Service Centres and New Towns. Very few people born overseas go to the Welsh Mining Towns or to Central Scotland.

Another way of describing this distribution of migrants would be to say that those born in the white Old Commonwealth and the

Table 8.9. Women with Children under Age Five Working Full-time and Part-time in Each Cluster

	London	Regional Service Centres	Resorts	Residential Suburbs	Industrial Suburbs	New Towns	Welsh Mining Towns	Engineering Towns I	Textile Towns	Engineering II	Heavy Engineering and Coal	Inner Conurbations	Central Scotland
Working:													
30 hours a week or more	124	61	55	59	73	68	98	66	166	94	105	101	120
8-30 hours	86	92	54	87	102	110	65	99	135	101	115	116	103
Under 8 hours	96	102	75	154	154	138	55	109	99	90	97	93	64

Table 8.10. Percentage of the Population Born Overseas, Mobility and Growth in Each Cluster

	London	Regional Service Centres	Resorts	Residential Suburbs	Industrial Suburbs	New Towns	Welsh Mining Towns	Engineering I	Textile Towns	Engineering II	Heavy Engineering and Coal	Inner Conurbations	Central Scotland
Proportion of population born in:													
Eire	179	54	57	71	57	67	15	47	74	116	31	125	63
Other European Countries	204	77	93	103	71	77	28	58	87	80	39	55	35
Old Commonwealth	198	108	125	162	77	114	15	46	46	61	29	42	71
Africa (New Commonwealth)	243	49	35	48	31	40	3	17	160	63	29	61	22
West Indies	246	40	10	14	12	14	0	44	57	61	56	109	2
India and Singapore	170	43	39	45	33	42	6	37	186	116	125	77	29
Pakistan	97	35	13	19	49	22	2	63	373	104	79	149	45
Other Oriental Countries	174	137	94	103	89	115	18	56	53	84	33	67	44
Total New Commonwealth	206	35	13	17	20	19	2	40	154	84	83	100	20
Growth of electorate 1955-70	90	99	107	130	116	160	86	96	92	116	104	90	96
People moving into Local Authority area in past 5 years	137	85	140	167	140	160	30	74	90	96	77	58	38

Far East tend to go to the towns of 'new Britain' to which the native born are also moving; while those born in the black New Commonwealth tend to go to the towns of 'traditional Britain' — the Textile Towns and the Inner Conurbations — slow growing or declining places which the native-born are leaving, where opportunities for work are generally less plentiful and less equally distributed among the social classes. Neither kind of migrant goes to the clusters which attract fewest people of all — the Welsh Mining Towns and Central Scotland. These differences may reflect the distribution of those industries which are being restructured to employ more machines and fewer workers at higher pay in 'new Britain', and those which resort to reductions in real wages and other devices in 'traditional Britain'.

Conclusion

This chapter shows that the growing and more prosperous towns which depend on the more modern forms of manufacturing, service industries and government tend to offer better opportunities for work to all social groups than those which depend on the older forms of manufacturing and mining industries. It suggests that other opportunities, such as those conferred by car ownership, follow from these characteristics of a town's industrial structure and reinforce them by extending people's access to the surrounding labour market. It is manual workers in general, and the least skilled in particular, who seem at first sight to gain most from the growth of the 'new Britain' and the replacement of older urban economies. The prosperous city is generally the more equal city.

But the relationship is not a simple one, for it is not every pattern of growth which has these benign results. The Resorts, for example, are growing fairly fast in population, but have fairly high levels of unemployment. Nor is every pattern of decline necessarily destructive: London is unique in having a rapidly falling population, yet behaving in many ways like a growing town.

Moreover the vast majority of manual workers are concentrated in the towns of 'traditional Britain' while a much higher proportion of the non-manual groups are concentrated in 'new Britain'. They are thus segregated in a way which reinforces inequality. And although the less skilled and the more vulnerable suffer most from the decline of old industrial towns, it does not necessarily follow that a faster national rate of growth would rescue them. Growth may occur, as so often before, in towns with relatively few poor and unskilled people. It may confer its main benefits on more prosperous towns and people, leaving the others to fall even further behind. Indeed, it may even be brought about by removing capital equipment and skilled workers from stagnant urban economies where they are badly needed to more productive places. Whether growth is equalising or unequalising will depend on how and where it occurs.

Which patterns of urban development are likely to be more constructive? Can such patterns be encouraged and, if so, how? If Britain succeeds in doing that, will the total volume of benign development be increased, or will it only be shifted from one place to another? We shall explore these questions in the next chapters.

9 Inner City Unemployment

Unanswered Questions
In the last two chapters we showed that the affluent New Towns, Residential Suburbs and Industrial Suburbs differ in many ways from the more deprived Inner Conurbations and the towns of Central Scotland. In this chapter we examine one aspect of these differences, unemployment, and the opportunities which various kinds of people have for getting jobs. Thus far we have presented little more than statistical associations among variables. Here we briefly outline various theories devised to explain patterns of unemployment, and test them with the evidence we have gathered.

We focus particularly on unemployment in the Inner Conurbations and Central Scotland. Policy documents often convey the impression that general agreement has been reached about the causes of what is sometimes called 'inner city' unemployment. But that is not true. Experts differ over fundamental questions such as whether the inner city should be treated as a 'local economy' with its own semi-autonomous labour market, or simply as a local arena in which national trends can be seen at work; and there is little agreement about the relative importance of factors, such as differences in rents, cyclical fluctuations in the market and changes in productivity, in determining whether inner city enterprises move, stay put, or close down.

As a result, studies of inner city areas often show merely that a particular area suffers severely from the decline of manufacturing and rising unemployment. They mention every possible reason for these problems and propose every kind of remedy from more bus lanes to discussions with the National Enterprise Board, but never explain which remedies are to solve which problems or why they are expected to do so.

Problems of Measurement
Unemployment itself is a complex concept, and changes in the unemployment rate can come about in many different ways. The 'stock' of

people unemployed may rise because more people are flowing into this category or because fewer people are flowing out. The inflow may increase because there are more redundancies, more people voluntarily quitting their jobs or more new entrants or re-entrants to the labour force. The outflow may fall because fewer unemployed people are being hired or fewer workers are withdrawing from the labour force. A given rate of unemployment may represent a small number of people who remain out of work for a long time, or a large number who find jobs quickly and turn over rapidly.

To make sense of such figures we must disaggregate them and examine the experience of particular groups. Interpreting the results then presents new problems. People may register as unemployed in the occupations they believe they stand the best chance of getting into, rather than those they last had or those for which they are best qualified. A decline in the demand for skilled labour may throw unskilled people out of work as the more skilled compete for their jobs, and the resulting figures may then misleadingly suggest that more unskilled jobs are needed. All these difficulties are compounded among women and, to a lesser extent, young people whose social security benefits give them less incentive to register as unemployed. Meanwhile unemployment figures for areas as small as some of the towns we have studied are notoriously unreliable because people tend to register as unemployed near their homes which may be a long way from their last jobs. Redundancies in the old docks, for example, may increase the figures for unemployment in places well outside the cities in which they stand.

We hope to explore some of these problems using data from the census of population rather than the Department of Employment. The census is derived from a questionnaire which goes to every household, not from people's decisions to register with the Employment Services: and all its figures are based on people's place of residence, not their place of work. The fairly large size of most of the urban areas used in our study helps to reduce the confusing effects of commuting and local migration.

We should also have looked at local changes in employment. Figures for change in employment by industry and occupation are usually more reliable and more illuminating than figures for unemployment. But even then we need to know why some industries are growing and most are declining. The usual approach to this question is to survey all the firms in an area and ask them why the number of jobs they offer has changed. The factors they mention are then ranked according to the number of times they appear. But such figures are difficult to interpret and may be positively misleading. Retailers, for example, may close because comprehensive redevelopment deprives them of cheap premises, and new ones are hard to come by. But this might not have been decisive if concentration and centralisation within retailing had not already driven many small shops close to bankruptcy. Ideally we should trace national trends in each industry, and then explore the roles which local firms play within their industries.

We have not been able to conduct such an exhaustive analysis, but we will try to set out the main theories which may explain the growth of unemployment in the inner cities and check them against the evidence we have been able to assemble. First we give some of the essential figures.

The Incidence of Unemployment

In 1971 4.0 per cent of the labour force in Britain were unemployed. Men were slightly more likely to be unemployed (with 4.2 per cent out of work) than women (for whom the figure was 3.7 per cent); but these comparisons underestimate the percentage of women who would work if jobs were available because many of them withdraw from the labour force when they have little chance of getting work. The youngest and oldest workers were more likely to be unemployed than those in the middle age band between 25 and 54. The highest figures were found among workers under twenty who (with 7.4 per cent out of work) suffered twice the unemployment rates of the 25-54 age group. In our urban areas unskilled manual workers (at 10.2 per cent) experienced about twice the unemployment rates of semi-skilled and skilled manual workers (with 4.6 and 4.4 per cent respectively), and these groups suffered about twice the rates experienced by the professional and managerial workers (2.0 per cent) and other non-manual workers (2.3 per cent). (See Table 8.2).

In the same year male unemployment rates in the Inner Conurbations and Central Scotland were 7.3 and 10.4 per cent respectively — well over the national average.* But in the New Towns, the Residential Suburbs and the New Industrial Suburbs the male unemployment rates were 1.9, 3.1 and 3.2 per cent respectively — much less than the national average. These and other figures are shown in Tables 9.1, 9.2 and 9.3.*

---

*The totals for each group recorded in the first two tables are national averages for Great Britain quoted above, not as in the previous and subsequent tables, the averages for all the towns in our cluster analysis. That is because these data were only available for local authority areas, not for the constituencies which formed the basis of our cluster analysis. Five towns had to be omitted from the computations which are summarised in these two tables because they do not correspond with any local authority area. They are Wokingham and East Kilbride (New Towns), Hazel Grove and Spelthorne (Residential Suburbs) and Pudsey (a New Industrial Suburb). These omissions are not likely to affect the argument which follows.

*Table 9.1. Unemployment Rates by Sex
for Selected Clusters of Towns: 1971*

	Unemployment rates by sex		As percentages of national averages for each sex		Women ÷ Men
	Men (1)	Women (2)	Men (3)	Women (4)	(3)/(4)
Central Scotland	10.4	5.1	249	137	1.82
Inner Conurbations	7.3	4.1	173	109	1.59
New Industrial Suburbs	3.2	3.4	76	89	0.85
Residential Suburbs	3.1	3.2	73	84	0.87
New Towns	1.9	2.9	45	78	0.58
National averages (Great Britain)	4.2	3.7	100	100	

(SOURCE: Census of Population, 1971.)

These three tables compare unemployment in two of the least prosperous and three of the most prosperous clusters of towns, and the experience in each town of different groups defined by sex, age and occupation. As in previous chapters, the figures show whether particular groups are doing better or worse in particular clusters, in comparison with their own kind elsewhere. As before, all groups do better in the more prosperous towns and all do worse in the less prosperous towns. But all groups do not benefit and suffer equally from urban prosperity and poverty.

The final columns of each table show the ratios of scores for the groups to be compared. The final column of Table 9.1, for example, shows that in the two impoverished clusters men experience heavier unemployment (in comparison with the scores for men in all towns) than women experience (in comparison with the scores for women in all towns). But in the three prosperous clusters men experience less unemployment in comparison with their national average than women do in comparison with theirs. Put more simply, Table 8.1 suggests that men suffer more than women from a poverty-stricken urban economy, and gain more from a prosperous one. But this finding must be treated

Table 9.2. *Unemployment Rates by Age for Selected*
Clusters of Towns, 1971

	Unemployment rates by age					
	15-19	20-24	25-54	55-64	65+	$\dfrac{15\text{-}19}{25\text{-}54}$
Central Scotland	11.91	11.09	8.03	6.03	2.81	1.48
Inner Conurbations	9.85	7.75	5.02	4.79	3.35	1.96
New Industrial Suburbs	6.07	3.87	2.33	3.58	2.91	2.61
Residential Suburbs	5.17	2.81	1.88	2.29	2.51	2.75
New Towns	6.39	4.31	2.72	2.57	3.85	2.35
National averages (Great Britain)	7.43	5.13	3.35	4.05	3.06	2.22

As percentages of the national unemployment rate for each age group

Central Scotland	160	216	240	149	92	0.67
Inner Conurbations	133	151	150	118	110	0.89
New Industrial Suburbs	82	75	70	88	95	1.18
Residential Suburbs	70	55	56	57	82	1.25
New Towns	86	84	81	63	126	1.06
National averages (Great Britain)	100	100	100	100	· 100	

(SOURCE: Census of Population, 1971.)

with caution because part of that difference — possibly all of it — could be due to women's reluctance to enter the labour market in places where jobs are hard to find. They may be more willing to describe themselves to census enumerators as unemployed in places where they expect to get a job quickly.

Table 9.2 suggests that all age groups suffer from urban poverty and all gain from urban prosperity, and in every kind of town the youngest workers, aged under 20, suffer more than the middle band aged 25-54. But these young workers suffer less of an additional disadvantage from urban poverty and gain less of a corresponding advantage from urban prosperity than the middle or 'prime' age band. It is those of prime age who suffer most and gain most from the depression or prosperity of their town. Table 9.3 suggests — as we showed in Chapter 8 — that all occupational groups gain from urban prosperity and all suffer from

Table 9.3. Unemployment Rates by Occupational Group for Selected
Clusters of Towns: 1971

(percentages of the average for each in all towns)

	Prof. and Managerial (1)	Other Non- Manual (2)	Skilled Manual (3)	Semi- Skilled (4)	Un- skilled (5)	Prof. ÷ Unskilled (1)/(5)	Non-manual ÷ Manual (1 + 2)/(3 + 4 + 5)
Central Scotland	157	161	210	209	228	0.69	0.74
Inner Conurbations	118	121	132	130	133	0.89	0.91
New Industrial Suburbs	93	79	63	61	64	1.45	1.37
Residential Suburbs	64	67	53	64	60	1.07	1.11
New Towns	75	62	52	52	48	1.56	1.34
All towns in cluster analysis	100	100	100	100	100	1.00	1.00

(SOURCE: Census of Population, 1971.)

urban poverty, but manual workers gain and suffer more than non-manual workers do.

Theories

Unemployment is particularly severe in Central Scotland and the Inner Conurbations. We will consider four kinds of theory which may help to explain why that is so: (i) those which emphasise the influence of the recession; (ii) those which emphasise the effects of 'dual' labour markets which make some workers, particularly concentrated in these towns, specially vulnerable to unemployment; (iii) those which emphasise the outward migration of capital and labour from these towns; and (iv) those which emphasise structural changes in the British economy particularly affecting industries concentrated in these towns. In reality all these processes are interdependent and cannot be clearly distinguished from each other. But it is analytically useful to examine them separately.

Recession

Two theories rely heavily on recession as a factor which tends to widen the differences between the unemployment rates for more skilled and less skilled workers. In the first Oi[1] points out that the costs of hiring, training, firing and replacing some kinds of workers are much higher than those for other workers. These 'quasi fixed costs' deter employers from sacking the workers concerned and encourage them to get rid of the less skilled and the less well organised instead. In a similar argument Reder suggests that during a recession firms raise the standards they demand from workers and the less able of the skilled workers filter down to oust less skilled workers from their jobs.[2]

Central Scotland and the Inner Conurbations contain high proportions of older producer goods industries, and they may also provide seedbeds for the growth of small marginal firms. Both are likely to be particularly vulnerable in a recession. These towns may also attract cyclically and seasonally unstable industries because, according to the Birmingham Inner Area Study, they contain neighbourhoods which provide 'a pool of cheap labour which is taken on and laid off according to the conditions of the wider economy'.[3] For all these reasons recession may make a greater impact upon them than upon other areas, and produce the pattern of heavy unemployment among less skilled workers observed in 1971 which was almost the trough of a recession.

These theories look less convincing when applied to women workers and young workers. Women and the young are said to provide a 'buffer stock' of labour which responds to cyclical fluctuations in demand. Being less well organised and less well trained than male manual workers in the prime of life (they have lower quasi-fixed costs) they will be the first to be fired in a recession. This would tend in depressed areas to produce a widening of age differences in unemployment and a narrowing of sex differences (because women normally have lower unemployment rates than men). Tables 9.1 and 9.2 show, however, that this is the reverse of what actually happens.

There is in fact little evidence to support cyclical theories of this kind. In Chapter 5 we argued that the main reason for the fall in employment in British industry is the long-term and long overdue reorganisation and re-equipment now going on. In many industries production has been increasing, not declining, as employment falls. Corkindale has shown that the experience of the Inner Conurbations varied during the years 1966-67 and 1970-71 when British unemployment rates increased sharply.[3] He gives figures for five of the cities in the clusters we have been examining. In Birmingham and Liverpool unemployment rates declined in relation to the national average during 1966-67. On Tyneside and in Glasgow there were declines in the relative rates of unemployment during 1970-71, and Leeds, Manchester and Liverpool only experienced small increases.

National figures for changes in unemployment by sex, age and skill also do not provide much support for a cyclical explanation of unemployment differentials. There appears to be a steady decline, unmarked by cyclical fluctuations, in the number of men in employment and an increase in the number of women. If recession were a dominant influence, the unemployment rates for women and others who constitute a large proportion of the 'buffer stock' of workers would fluctuate with the trade cycle. The Department of Employment has shown that young workers experienced the fastest increase in the rate of unemployment as the cyclical approach would predict, but this occurred after 1968 rather than in 1966 when the first major increase in unemployment occurred.[4] This study also found that in general 'the trend in unemployment among labourers has moved closely in parallel with the trend for all unemployed men'.[5] Unemployment among administrative, professional and technical workers followed the same pattern. All this suggests that recession is not the major factor producing unemployment in these cities.

The dual labour market

A second group of theories which have been used to explain the high rates of unemployment in cities of the kind we are studying relies on the concept of a dual labour market. Unemployment, it is said, is concentrated in a secondary labour market where wages are low, and work is unskilled and unpleasant. Partly because people cannot stick at these jobs for long, labour turnover is high. Many of the small firms, the labour intensive industries and the trades responding to fashion and the seasons which tend to concentrate in the inner city operate in this secondary market. Others are attracted there in search of the kind of labour they need. The Community Development Projects drew conclusions of this kind in a study of five older industrial areas in which they argue that 'small marginal firms will actively seek out areas where such workers are to be found (the unskilled, the unemployed, etc.) and they also look for the more vulnerable and less organised sectors of the work force such as immigrants and women'.[6] Many women, young workers and immigrants are restricted to the secondary labour market because of policies of discrimination and a lack of bargaining power.

Little work has been carried out to test these theories in Britain. Bosanquet and Doeringer[7] have produced some evidence that the labour market is stratified in this way at a national level, but little research has been done at the inner city level. This is a pity because as manufacturing and larger enterprises decline there, small labour intensive firms will probably grow relatively more important in the inner city economy. Indeed, some see the promotion of small enterprise as a solution to inner city problems. If they succeed in that aim, theories about a dual labour market may grow more relevant for these cities in future.

But our evidence shows that such theories will not take us far. If they were generally valid for these cities, unemployment would be particularly high there among the unskilled, women, the youngest workers, and others who play a large part in the secondary labour force. Table 9.3 shows that unskilled workers do indeed suffer particularly heavy unemployment in the towns of Central Scotland and the Inner Conurbations. But their experience is much the same as that of skilled and semi-skilled manual workers: their disadvantages in these places seem to be those of the whole manual working class, not those of a secondary labour force. Meanwhile, Tables 9.1 and 9.2 show that women and the youngest workers suffer not more, but less, severe unemployment in relation to their own kind elsewhere than men and workers in the prime of life. Dual labour market theories, at least in their simpler forms, cannot explain the pattern of unemployment in these cities.

Local disequilibrium

A third group of theories, which have become less popular as national rates of unemployment have increased, attribute the particularly high rates in these cities to a mismatch between the location of jobs and the location of workers. The mismatch is said to arise because jobs and workers move to other local labour markets at different rates. Thus unemployment in one local labour market would be matched by unfilled vacancies in another, and solutions are sought through government intervention to bring the work to the workers, or the workers to the work.

The factors which are usually said to have made the inner parts of the biggest cities less attractive as a location for firms include: (i) a shortage of land and adequate premises; (ii) high prices for land and premises; (iii) a shortage of particular types of skilled labour; (iv) road congestion; and (v) state intervention in the form of land use restrictions and comprehensive redevelopment schemes in the inner city, coupled with regional policies which are designed to make other areas more attractive.

If jobs move out of the inner city in a reasonably random order, but some workers are less mobile than others, it will be these workers — usually thought to be the least skilled, the youngest, the oldest, and women — who suffer the highest rates of unemployment. Conversely, in prosperous towns to which industry is moving, these less mobile workers should do particularly well. Their immobility may be reinforced by such things as the criteria used to allocate local authority houses — criteria, giving great weight to time spent on the waiting list, which compel people for whom the authorities offer the only hope of rehousing to stay in a town once they have registered their names on its list. Later, when rehoused, they may find it much harder to exchange houses with tenants of other authorities than an owner-occupier would find it to sell his home and buy another elsewhere.

Our evidence gives little support to these theories of mismatch. In depressed towns women and the youngest workers suffer, not more, but less, severe unemployment in relation to their group elsewhere. Men in the prime of life, who are generally assumed to be more mobile, do better in prosperous places and worse in depressed places in relation to their own group. Table 9.2 shows that older workers, over the age of 54, do better, by comparison with workers of prime age, in the more depressed places than in the more prosperous places. Moreover, because they stress the disadvantages of the Inner Conurbations, these theories suggest that unemployment there should be worse than it is in the towns of Central Scotland which, apart from Glasgow, are much smaller, and do not stand at the heart of great conurbations[8] — or at least it should take different patterns. But the unemployment we show in Tables 9.1, 9.2 and 9.3 takes similar patterns in the two clusters, and is not better but much worse in Central Scotland than the Inner Conurbations.

The main reason for the loss of jobs in these cities is not the movement of enterprises, but their death or decline, as we shall show. Among the firms which do move, many reduce their labour force in transit. Their reason for moving is often not so much the character of a particular area as the fact that movement enables them to introduce new technology and hire new workers with different skills or at lower wages without costly retraining, regrading and industrial conflict.

The one point at which our evidence does give some support to these theories is in comparisons between manual and non manual workers. For non-manual workers there is much less difference in unemployment rates between the declining old industrial towns and the new, expanding towns. That is probably because they are better able than manual workers to move to prosperous places and to commute to them from homes elsewhere, and the supply of labour is thus better matched with demands for it.

Restructuring industry

Finally we come to the fourth kind of theory, already outlined in

Chapter 5, which would attribute high unemployment in these cities mainly to the reorganisation and re-equipment of industries which are heavily concentrated there. It does not dismiss the importance of the recession, dual labour markets, or locational factors such as high rents, but relegates them to the role of catalysts rather than fundamental causes of the growth of unemployment. The fundamental cause is the concentration in the Inner Conurbations and Central Scotland of older industries, plants and processes which are being rationalised in a bid to raise productivity.

The Association of Metropolitan Authorities has found that all large conurbations, except London, rely heavily on industries which are declining on a national scale.[9] Our cluster analysis showed that the Inner Conurbations and Central Scotland contain higher than average proportions of the main industries which were declining between 1966 and 1971 — distribution, textiles, food, drink and tobacco, metal goods, construction and transport and communication. Together these accounted for approximately 50 per cent of the national decline in employment between 1966 and 1971.[10] The Inner Conurbations also contain a higher than average proportion of the vehicles industry, and Central Scotland contains a higher than average proportion of the ship-building industry, both of which accounted for a large proportion of the national decline in male employment between 1966 and 1971.

Various studies suggest that industrial reorganisation and re-equipment are now among the dominant changes shaping the economies of British towns. In their study of the electronics industry, Doreen Massey and Richard Meegan found that firms were adopting more capital intensive methods of production.[11] Within this reduced total of required labour, there were fewer skilled men and more semi-skilled women proportionately. These firms often moved to new places in order to reorganise with the minimum resistance from the original, male-dominated labour force. Similarly, the Canning Town Community Development Project discovered that fifteen, mainly multinational firms accounted for 75 per cent of the jobs in their inner urban area.[12] Six of these companies (all multinationals) accounted for 75 per cent of the jobs lost in the area between 1966 and 1972. These companies were not failing; they were relatively profitable in comparison with the national average. But the sectors in which they operate require a high return on capital, which is why they have been compelled to reorganise.

Things do not always go so well for the firms in such areas. The Birmingham Inner Area Study found that the main reason for the loss of jobs there was not the emigration of firms but their death.[13] Most of the jobs lost were in large firms closing because of general trading conditions — not because of local conditions such as high rents or redevelopment.

How would these development affect different kinds of workers? The skills required by the growing industries differ from those lost in the declining industries, and within industries new technologies have called for changed skills, as we explained in Chapter 5. Between 1961 and 1971, both these processes worked in the same direction. There was an enormous increase in the demands for non-manual workers, particularly for women, in occupations such as routine office work, personal service, teaching and nursing, and a massive decline in the demand for manual workers from which men suffered the heaviest losses.

All this suggests that when compared with cities full of new expanding industries, unemployment in Central Scotland and the Inner Conurbations — cities typical of old industrial Britain — should be particularly high among men, among people in the prime of life who may find it harder than the youngest workers to switch to new, expanding industries, and among manual, rather than non-manual, workers.

The first prediction is confirmed by Table 9.1. Men suffer more than women, in comparison with their own sex elsewhere, in Central Scotland and the Inner Conurbations; and they benefit more in the expanding clusters — particularly the most rapidly growing cluster of New Towns. The pattern is probably reinforced by the fact that many of the growing occupations for women — in clerical and secretarial work, for example — are concentrated in the Inner Conurbations, partly offsetting their lost opportunities in these declining labour markets.

The outcome for different age groups is more complicated. Wherever possible, employers seem to have reduced their labour forces by not hiring new workers and waiting for natural wastage to take its toll. Thus school leavers — girls as well as boys — bore the brunt of the decline in employment which occurred after 1966. Because many responded by not leaving school the increase in unemployment among younger workers, though severe, was much less than it might have been. But once that general, national bias against younger workers has been taken into account, if comparisons are made between growing and declining towns, workers in the prime of life, between 25 and 54, suffered relatively more than younger workers and older workers, as we would expect. Conversely, prime age workers benefited more than the youngest workers in the more prosperous towns.

The patterns for different occupations are also complex but broadly conform to our expectations. As predicted, the skilled and semi-skilled manual workers suffer more from decline and benefit more from prosperity than do the non-manual workers. But comparisons between the unskilled and the more skilled manual workers show no consistent pattern. Their failure to show the expected patterns is probably due to several reasons. Our evidence deals only with the crudest kind of hardship — unemployment. It tells us nothing about lost incomes, skills and status. As skilled jobs disappear, those who hold them are rarely unemployed for long: they take less skilled jobs and probably describe themselves to census enumerators as members of their new occupations. Meanwhile it is the unskilled at the bottom of the labour market who are most likely to be squeezed out of work altogether. Skilled manual workers may also be better able than the unskilled to quit declining towns and move to expanding ones. The Inner Conurbations and Central Scotland also have higher than average proportions of workers in Construction, and Transport and Communications. Together these industries accounted for 45 per cent of the decline in unskilled employment between 1966 and 1971.

Conclusions

The four theories we have examined cannot be as sharply distinguished from each other as this brief formulation of the ideas may suggest. But when confronted with our evidence, the fourth, in which the restructuring of industry plays a central part, emerges as the strongest.

Research done thus far on the economies of cities describes many of the problems which urban planners are beginning to contend with — problems, essentially, of growing needs and declining resources — but it fails to explain them or to offer convincing solutions. For that we shall need better theories tested by more relevant evidence. We particularly need a better understanding of the parts played by different industries within the rapidly changing national and international economies, and the parts played by local enterprises within those industries. Already the evidence presented in this chapter takes us a little further.

The problems of the most depressed cities are not due simply to recession. Adverse trading conditions will sometimes be the last straw leading to closures and lay-offs; but the industries and enterprises affected will usually have more fundamental weaknesses. The problems of a marginal or secondary labour force, described in theories about dual labour markets, have always afflicted the larger depressed cities more severely than growing, prosperous towns full of new industries. But these problems are neither a new nor a wholly distinctive feature of declining urban economies, and they do not explain their main difficulties — although they may serve to warn us of the dangers inherent in urban policies which rely too heavily on the kind of small firms which operate in secondary labour markets.

The main problems which must be resolved before the economies of Britain's most depressed cities can be revived are a product of history. Large parts of the industries represented there are losing ground all over the world. Some must be drastically reorganised if they are to survive in this country. Many of the industries now due for reorganisation grew up at the same time and are thus heavily concentrated in cities which prospered during the period of their growth. To make these industries more competitive and more profitable — and many are succeeding to some extent in doing that, often with massive help from the Government, will not necessarily create more jobs. More often than not, reorganisation reduces labour costs and the incomes of local workers, and increases unemployment.

These are sombre conclusions. But this chapter has more cheerful implications too. The main problems of the depressed cities are national, not local, in origin. They are not mainly due to local conditions such as high rents, cramped sites and road congestion. It follows that there is nothing inherently or permanently destructive about the environment these cities offer. Neighbourhoods which were once a setting for innovative, expanding enterprises could recapture their previous prosperity.

To bring about a revival of these urban economies will call for investment designed as much to use and develop the talents of the local labour force as to increase the return on capital. That cannot be expected of investors who respond only to present market motivations. Public authorities will therefore have to play a larger and more sophisticated part in this field; and policies for different industries must be more closely coordinated. Where in order to modernise an enterprise there must be a heavy loss of jobs to achieve a sufficient return on capital, there must also be compensating investment in labour intensive forms of production. If that cannot be achieved, reorganisation may have to wait. Town planners will have a part to play in formulating policies of this kind and putting them into practice.

10 Middle England

In the last chapter we traced in Central Scotland and the Inner Conurbations the destructive impact of some of the major changes now going on in the British economy. We might have shown similar forces at work in the Welsh Mining Towns. To clarify the problems of these depressed towns we contrasted them with more prosperous and rapidly growing places: the New Towns, the Residential and the New Industrial Suburbs. Together, these depressed and prosperous places provide a map of economic changes now proceeding on a national scale: they are products of history, typifying what we described as 'new' and 'old' Britain. While something can be done at a local scale and in the short term to help the depressed places, any major change in their prospects will call for larger and longer term developments on a national scale. Likewise the prosperity of the more buoyant places, because it also reflects national trends, can neither easily nor readily be multiplied across Britain: the demands for the goods and services supplied by the leafy suburbs and the new towns cannot be limitlessly extended – at least not in the short run. If that is the end of the story, the scope for local urban-scale planning is likely to be very limited. In this chapter we consider whether there may be more hopeful lessons to be learnt from other less extreme but more typical examples of Britain's urban structure.

The six extreme clusters mentioned in the previous paragraph account for only 55 towns – little more than one third of the 154 towns in our analysis. They and the three clusters with distinctive characteristics which place them at the top of the dendogram on page 101 (London, the Regional Service Centres and the Resorts) together account for little more than half of the places we have studied. The other half amount to 71 towns (or 74 if the Welsh Mining Towns are included) which fall into one 'family' of four clusters in the middle of the dendogram. These are Cluster 8, Engineering I (Doncaster and Stockport being the most typical of these); 9, the Textile Towns (for example Bolton and Oldham); 10, Engineering II (for example Swindon and Gloucester); and 11, Heavy Engineering and Coal (for example Walsall and Farnworth). They are described and mapped (see Chapter 7, pages 95-7) as predominantly working class, English, manufacturing towns, much like each other in many ways. The dendogram clearly shows this.

Cluster 10

If there is scope for shaping or reshaping the course of urban development by planning and managing it at a local scale, then it may be among these towns that such opportunities are to be found. In this chapter we shall concentrate particularly on Cluster 10, a group of fourteen towns to which we gave the unrevealing name of Engineering II.

These towns are interesting for several reasons. They have rather more than their share of the nation's more vulnerable people. Proportionately they have more manual workers, and more of the semi-skilled and unskilled in particular, than most towns; and they have fewer non-manual workers, and fewer professional and managerial workers in particular. The proportions of their workers possessing 'A' level certificates, degrees or similar qualifications are below the national averages (see Tables 7.1 and 7.2). As Table 8.10 shows, they have rather more immigrants than other towns, particularly from Eire and the New Commonwealth. And they have more large families and more one-parent families than most towns, as Table 10.1 illustrates. It is not surprising if things generally go well in the Residential and Industrial Suburbs, the New Towns and the Resorts, because they have less than their share of the vulnerable groups: it is more interesting if things don't go too badly in towns which have larger than average proportions of these groups.

Their lack of clearly distinctive character is another interesting feature of these fourteen towns. They are not strongly contrasted with other types of towns. Such contrasts usually imply a functional link: the Suburbs and New Towns, for example, differ from the Inner Conurbations because they have taken younger and more skilled and successful people from them; they are opposite sides of the same coin. You cannot multiply the advantages of one without multiplying the handicaps of the other. Cluster 10 is not like that. These towns do not depend heavily on one age group, as do the Resorts which are full of retired people. They do not depend on one industry, as do the Mining and Textile Towns. They are not confined to one urban type, like the Suburbs, or to one part of the country, like the Welsh, Scottish and Textile

Table 10.1. Rankings of Clusters by Indicators of Vulnerability

Unskilled		Large families (2 adults, 5 or more dep. children)		One-parent families (1 adult, 2 or more dep. children)		New Commonwealth born		People aged 15-25		People aged 65 or more	
Central Scotland	154	Central Scotland	202	Central Scotland	151	London	206	Central Scotland	107	Resorts	184
Inner Conurbations	130	Inner Conurbations	146	Inner Conurbations	139	Textile Towns	154	Inner Conurbations	105	Regional Service Centres	111
Textile Towns	115	Engineering II	130	Textile Towns	124	Inner Conurbations	100	Regional Service Centres	104	Welsh Mining Towns	109
Welsh Mining Towns	113	Textile Towns	112	Engineering II	116	Engineering II	84	Engineering II	102	Textile Towns	107
Heavy Engineering and Coal	107	Heavy Engineering and Coal	108	Regional Service Centres	97	Heavy Engineering and Coal	83	London	102	Engineering I	104
Engineering I	104	New Towns	89	London	88	Engineering I	40	Textile Towns	99	London	101
Engineering II	101	Regional Service Centres	83	Engineering I	86	Regional Service Centres	35	Heavy Engineering and Coal	99	Inner Conurbations	98
Regional Service Centres	101	Engineering I	79	Heavy Engineering and Coal	83	Central Scotland	20	New Towns	97	New Industrial Suburbs	97
London	88	Welsh Mining Towns	76	New Towns	82	New Industrial Suburbs	20	Engineering I	96	Central Scotland	89
New Industrial Suburbs	70	London	73	Welsh Mining Towns	72	New Towns	19	Wales	93	Residential Suburbs	89
Resorts	60	New Industrial Suburbs	69	Resorts	72	Residential Suburbs	17	New Industrial Suburbs	92	Heavy Engineering and Coal	88
New Towns	56	Residential Suburbs	61	New Industrial Suburbs	65	Resorts	13	Residential Suburbs	87	Engineering II	79
Residential Suburbs	35	Resorts	41	Residential Suburbs	47	Welsh Mining Towns	2	Resorts	79	New Towns	64

See note to Table 7.1.

clusters. They range from Teesside and Ormskirk in the North to Gosport, and Rochester and Chatham in the South. They include freestanding towns like Peterborough and Gloucester, old suburbs like Stretford and newer ones like Eton and Slough, old ports like Grimsby and newer ones like Thurrock, and centres of the motor industry like Coventry and Luton. Thus if they do have desirable characteristics it is less obvious than it would be for towns of a more uniform type that there is a limit to the number of such places the country can sustain.

How desirable are they? Table 8.5 shows that, depite their considerable concentrations of vulnerable people, these towns had marginally lower than average unemployment rates. This may be partly because their opportunities for work were extended by car ownership and travel to work by car which were both distinctly higher than average for all occupational groups, as Tables 8.7 and 8.8 show. Our data do not reveal the housing conditions of particular social groups, only the conditions in particular kinds of towns. But Table 7.1 shows that people in these towns were more likely to live in houses equipped with all the standard amenities, and Table 7.2 shows they were marginally less likely to be overcrowded than people in other towns. In the next chapter we will show that the attainments of their eleven-year-old children in reading and mathematics — particularly those in the middle and lower social groups — were rather higher than the social composition and character of these towns would lead us to expect.

These patterns can be summed up by looking at one of the most basic of opportunities — the opportunity for getting married. In the predominantly working class towns of 'old' Britain, people tend to marry at younger ages than they do in the more prosperous towns of 'new' Britain. Early marriage may in some ways reinforce the handicaps of these communities. It may make it harder to pursue extended training before starting in a full-time job. If it leads to earlier parenthood, that makes it more difficult to save money for the down payment on a house, or for the car which could extend opportunities for work, recreation and other activities. For these and other reasons young parents may have greater difficulties in rearing their children: research reported in the next chapter shows that a child's success at school is related to the age of his mother when he was born. In all classes the children of older mothers tend to do better.

It is in the towns of 'new' Britain, where the proportion who marry early is low, that the proportion who are married by the age of forty is highest. Marriage rates for men and women under 20 and for those aged between 35 and 40 are compared in Table 10.2. It shows major

Table 10.2. Marriage Rates by Age in Each Cluster

	London	Regional Service Centres	Resorts	New Industrial Suburbs	Residential Suburbs	New Towns	Welsh Mining Towns	Engineering I	Textile Towns	Engineering II	Heavy Engineering and Coal	Inner Conurbations	Central Scotland
Age:													
15-20 Men	74	99	80	82	40	67	151	109	137	99	133	121	131
Women	86	104	91	95	53	88	129	109	125	111	120	101	101
35-40 Men	96	100	101	105	107	109	99	102	102	103	102	97	99
Women	96	99	97	104	104	106	103	103	102	104	104	99	98

differences which narrow with advancing age. Despite their slow start, the New Industrial and Residential Suburbs and New Towns — the 'new Britain', Clusters 4, 5 and 6 — end at the top of the marriage rates among the 35-40 year olds. That is partly because they recruit married couples from the older towns. On the other hand, the Welsh Mining and Textile Towns, the Inner Conurbations and Central Scotland — the 'old Britain', Clusters 7, 9, 12 and 13 — have high early marriage rates but generally fall behind the other clusters in the middle age groups where marriage rates attain their peak.

Cluster 10 starts among the teenagers with high marriage rates for women and average rates for men, but it ends in the older age group with high figures too, little short of the scores for 'new' Britain towns. Heavy Engineering Towns follow a similar pattern.

We have shown that the towns in Cluster 10 are in most respects typical working class communities with considerable numbers of the vulnerable groups to be found in such communities. Yet they seem to have achieved better and somewhat more equally distributed living standards and educational attainments than towns of that kind usually attain. How has that been done? Can the achievement be more widely imitated? Should it be? These are the increasingly speculative questions to which we now turn.

Patterns of Growth

The main characteristic which distinguishes Cluster 10 from other working class towns is the high rate at which its populations are growing. This stands out clearly in Table 8.10. Clusters 6 and 5 — the New Towns and Residential Suburbs — were growing fastest of all. Then comes Cluster 10, followed by Cluster 4 — the New Industrial Suburbs. Next come the Resorts (Cluster 3) and the Heavy Engineering Towns (Cluster 11). All the other towns we described as predominantly working class (those represented by Clusters 7 to 13) are growing more slowly or declining in population. Growth in population is not a separate causal agent — a miracle additive which can be distinguished from other characteristics of a town. It is an integral feature of the urban economy which follows from, and helps to create, the general enlargement of work, earnings and opportunities in general. We have shown that it is usually associated with an extension and equalisation of opportunities for work and for the ownership and use of cars, with the improvement of housing conditions, high rates of marriage and family formation among the middle aged groups and a younger demographic structure. These are only its more obviously measurable associations.

To say that demographic growth, by itself, causes the patterns we have observed in Cluster 10 would be misleading because demographic growth does not operate by itself. It is the general expansion — industrial, commercial and demographic — of their urban economies, including their public services, which, we believe, has helped the towns in Cluster 10 to achieve the good things which have happened there.

There is in the short run little scope for increasing the nation's rate of demographic growth and many would not want to do so. It has been declining since 1964 and may fall below replacement rate for some years. Thus it would be rash to assert that the patterns of development to be seen in Cluster 10 can be reproduced all over the country. Some would conclude that such patterns can perhaps be redistributed geographically, but cannot be enlarged in total. That is probably too pessimistic: the demographic element is not the only strand in the pattern, and is unlikely to be the most important one. Economic and social development and progress towards a more equal distribution of opportunities are generally easier to achieve in towns with growing populations, but they are not impossible elsewhere.

The industrial character of these towns and the high levels of employment which that industry has brought them probably play a more fundamental part in the story than demographic growth. Thus a more serious constraint on the dissemination of the patterns to be seen in this cluster may be found in their industrial base

We do not know enough about it to explore the problem far. Many industries are represented among these towns, but modern forms of light engineering probably predominate. Luton and Coventry depend heavily on the motor industry, for example, and so presumably do Thurrock (close to Dagenham), Slough (close to another Ford plant) and Peterborough (producer of diesel engines). In Swindon, too, about one-fifth of the workers are in the motor industry.[1] Depression in this industry must mean that some of these towns are now less prosperous than they were in 1971 when our data were gathered. We may, in effect, be dealing with a non-spatial region of the British economy — the places where the more rapidly growing manufacturing industries have taken root. If so, the scope for multiplying these patterns of urban development depends heavily on our success, at urban and at national scales, in developing these and similar forms of production. That may not be easy, but it is not impossible — and developments originating at urban scale can help to bring the achievement about.

Scope for Planning

For local planners and their councils we can offer a more confident conclusion. Given a reasonably favourable location, and sustained and effective political leadership, a city which appears to be heading for economic and social decline can be transformed into a buoyant urban economy of the kind which Cluster 10 typifies. Swindon is the clearest example of a town which was transformed in this way. Peterborough, whose planned expansion began later, may prove to be another.

The story of Swindon's expansion has been told elsewhere.[2] Michael Harloe's account is particularly revealing. Created in its modern form by the Great Western Railway, Swindon fell into economic and demographic decline in the 1930s as the railways declined. Briefly recovering during the war, which brought industries of all kinds to its empty workshops, the town's economy seemed likely to decay again in peacetime. But thanks largely to a great town clerk and his council which gave bipartisan support for expansion under the Town Development Act of 1952, Swindown was transformed. Job opportunities expanded enormously, even faster for women than for men, and unemployment rates fell to very low levels. Earnings, which had been lagging behind the national averages, overtook them. Housing conditions improved, and the proportion of households owning their own homes and owning cars soon surpassed the national average. Population grew rapidly, and the town acquired new roads and shops; a civic centre with a theatre, concert hall and library were built; so too were new schools, a college of further education and a hospital — most of them products of the expansion scheme. The proportion of workers in professional, managerial and other non-manual jobs increased. Delinquency and other signs of stress remained very low.

Swindon's successful development was due partly to deliberate policies for the expansion and diversification of manufacturing industries and service trades offering jobs for men and women with a wide range of middle-grade skills. Investors were recruited from all parts of the country, and pressures to tie the expansion scheme too closely to London's needs were skilfully resisted. Housing was built to match the demands generated by this growing labour market. Swindon was determined not to build the segregated 'overspill' estates for newcomers, let at specially high rents, which other town expansion schemes have provided. Newcomers were offered council houses scattered throughout estates built for everyone else in the town. Houses were built for sale, and before long one-third of the newcomers who started in council houses moved on to buy their own homes, leaving vacancies for their successors.

This achievement was 'planned' in the sense that it would never have happened without the political commitment and flair of a small number of councillors and officials and a great deal of hard labour by the borough's senior staff. Local government, backed by the London County Council, the Ministry of Housing and eventually a more reluctant Wiltshire County Council, created the opportunity and impetus for growth, to which private enterprise then added its massive contribution.

But conventional town planning skills played little part in the story. Indeed it was Swindon's constant and generally successful endeavour to prevent the London County Council's planners – then one of the most famous teams of architect planners to be found anywhere in the world – from designing or building any of the expansion. Planning consultants were hired – sometimes to fend off other potential intruders – but powers were not delegated to them. The results were sometimes inelegant, as Swindon people would admit, but far worse environments have been created by more highly qualified professionals. Meanwhile, from London's point of view, it is clear that the Swindon expansion scheme in relation to its costs, made a bigger contribution to helping Londoners in need of housing than was made by the more prestigious new towns (which were more expensive and less likely to recruit people with housing needs) or by other town expansion schemes in which the London County Council played a bigger part. (Other expanded towns were rather more likely than Swindon to recruit Londoners with housing needs, but they were smaller and more slow moving projects.)

We conclude that with favourable circumstances – amongst which the key *people* are even more important than the advantages of particular locations – urban development of the kind found in Cluster 10 can be deliberately brought about. Harloe's and Levin's books make it clear that the crucial processes and skills for achieving this development are political and, in a broad and creative sense, administrative. The design skills which form the core of most town planners' training played only a small part in the story. But much – probably most – of the productive investment which forms the basis for this development serves wider markets; and most of this growth would probably have occurred somewhere in any case. Thus Swindon's revival has probably been achieved partly at the cost of decay in other towns.

The 'Good City'
We have yet to consider whether we *want* more towns of the sort which Cluster 10 typifies. This is a question of values to which no authoritative

answer could be given, but that does not make it less important. Our data throw little light on the quality of life in these or other towns: more intensive research is now needed on the history and character of communities typifying contrasting patterns of development. But common knowledge and a little speculation may suggest some of the points which such research would explore.

We have stressed that the economic opportunities offered by these towns are better than those usually found in communities of their social composition. But we believe their advantages are not only materialistic: in the next chapter we show that children in these towns do rather better in school than their social origins would lead us to expect. The politics of these towns tend, we suspect, to be rather more robust, more open to public debate and the influence of newcomers, and probably less corrupt than in some other towns. They probably lack entrenched political élites because migration, in and out, is rather larger among all socio-economic groups than it is in most towns. The public services of these towns are sometimes very good. Some have had long periods of Labour Party rule, sometimes with innovative results: Luton was a pioneer in reorganising secondary education with its sixth-form colleges. (Affluent workers in modern industries probably know better than most how the old-fashioned secondary modern school deprived their children of opportunities.) Coventry has been a pioneer in education and town planning. Swindon's expansion was brought about largely by a Labour Council which was wise enough to seek Conservative and Independent support for that scheme, thus keeping it out of party politics. The Labour Party cannot be complacent in these towns for it has no monopoly there. If all clusters are ranked according to their propensity to vote Conservative in the general election of 1970, ranging from the Residential Suburbs and Resorts on the right to Central Scotland and Heavy Engineering on the left, Cluster 10 stands at the very middle of the order.

Together, these towns might be described as 'middle England', and they also have some of the less attractive features that title suggests: few good bookshops, few buildings listed for preservation, no entry in the *Good Food Guide*, no 'starred' restaurants in the *Egon Ronay Guide*, and no hotel which receives the distinction of a 'rosette' in the *Automobile Association's Guide*. Although some have good technical colleges, only one has a university — and that had to be called the University of Warwick, not Coventry (and most of its teachers appear to live in and around Warwick and Leamington Spa). In short, these are not places in which the groups dominating Britain and its 'establishment' spend much time or give much thought to. One of the most hallowed institutions of upper class Britain happens, rather accidentially, to stand in one of these towns (Eton and Slough), but its alumni rarely settle in such places. The Poet Laureate conveyed the establishment's view of middle England when he wrote during the war, 'Come friendly bombs and fall on Slough. . . .'³ Meanwhile the establishment's left wing is usually more attracted by working class communities which have the glamour of heavy industry, poverty, slums and political militancy: the affluent working class they find less appealing.

Nevertheless, these towns may be a portent for the future – a foretaste of the prosperous, equal, fully employed world we are trying to create. If so, they are a good beginning: having a job, a car, a good house and decent schools for your children are starting points for the good life. But they are only starting points.

11 Education: Cause or Effect?

Although we have tried to place our findings in a historical context, briefly explaining how urban patterns evolve over time, most of our evidence comes from the Census and thus provides no more than a static picture – snapshots of cities at one moment in their history. To gain a better understanding of different patterns of urban development, their causes and effects, we need longitudinal studies tracing the experience of different kinds of places and different kinds of people over time. That is what we attempt to provide, if only in a preliminary experimental way, in the next two chapters.

Do children develop differently in different places? Do their home towns influence their aspirations and attainments? In this chapter we begin to explore these complicated questions by asking about children's educational attainments.

Sources and Methods

The chapter is based on work done at the National Children's Bureau by Hilary Robinson, Peter Gorbach and Peter Wedge who made a special analysis, in collaboration with us, of the attainment of children in the Bureau's National Child Development Study (NCDS) which is tracing the development of some 16,000 children born in 1958.[1] Their findings, which will be published soon, are already available from the Bureau[2] and we will not try to summarise them here. We draw only on those parts of their work which are particularly relevant to our own research. Although the evidence comes from a longitudinal study, this first instalment deals with children and towns at one point in time. Its authors hope it may be possible to follow up these children and look again later at them and the towns in which they live. We must briefly explain methods of research before presenting our findings, but readers who are not interested in methodological problems may prefer to skip to the next section of this chapter, starting on page 147.

Those working on the NCDS considered various aspects of child development which might be compared from place to place. They abandoned the idea of studying variations in health. The most reliable measures available were for the heights and weights of children, but variations were small when large groups were compared and the influence of heredity discounted. They were also difficult to interpret. Long ago, taller and heavier generally meant healthier; but in a more affluent society that can no longer be assumed. The Bureau therefore focussed on education, taking two measures as criteria: reading and mathematical attainments, both at the age of eleven. That age was chosen because the Bureau had made a successful 'sweep' of their cohort of children in 1969, not too distant in time from the 1971 Census which provides most of our data. In all the analyses from which we quote, the attainments of the groups of children to be compared are expressed as a positive or negative deviation, measured in fractions of a year, from the average attainment of the whole national cohort at about age eleven. Thus the best reading age recorded in Table 11.1 is 0.92 for children in the Resorts, and the worst is -0.52, for children in the Heavy Engineering Towns. This means that on average the children in the Resorts were 11 months ahead and the children in Heavy Engineering Towns were 6 months behind the national mean — a range of 17 months in average reading ages between children in the top and bottom clusters.

The NCDS can be used to compare the eleven regions of Britain, and the local education authorities (they were administrative counties and county boroughs in 1969) — provided the authorities in question had children in the NCDS cohort. Many of the towns we studied were not county boroughs in 1969. In some of those which were, an exact comparison with our areas was impossible because we based our study on constituencies for which the boundaries were not always coterminous with those of the boroughs. Towns in the NCDS analysis were allocated to clusters, using our methods and allowing for the change in cluster means brought about by excluding some of the towns originally included in our study. In the course of this operation some towns were shifted to clusters other than those to which we had allocated them. Losses due to these and other problems cut down the clusters of towns assembled from NCDS data to 9. These approximately matched 9 of our 13 clusters, and included 81 of our 154 towns.

The clusters of towns included in the NCDS analysis are genuinely distinctive, but can they be reliably equated with ours? The Bureau's authors made various comparisons between towns with and without the problems of boundary overlap, and found very little difference between the two groups of towns or the attainments of children in similar clusters. They examined all the clusters emerging from their analysis and only found one with characteristics which differed significantly from the clusters of the same names which we used. Their Heavy Engineering group of towns contained more single women who were at work but fewer married women workers than ours did. In other respects their clusters and ours resembled each other very closely. The NCDS Central Scotland cluster only retains two of the six towns in our cluster, but one of these is Glasgow which dominates both their version of the cluster and ours by virtue of its size. (The other NCDS town is Dundee.)

It is the clusters missing from this analysis which leave a glaring gap. Because it is based on local education authorities which were county boroughs, the NCDS represents large and long-established cities; smaller towns, suburbs and more recent urban growth generally fall into the administrative counties which cannot be matched with our towns. Thus Clusters 4, 5, 6 and 7 are omitted. The first three of these are among the four most rapidly growing clusters, and among the four clusters with the largest proportions of professional and managerial workers and the smallest proportions of unskilled manual workers. Most of the towns we described as 'new Britain' — rapidly growing, southern, service-industry towns — are missing from this analysis. The clusters remaining that are nearest to this description in the NCDS analysis are the Resorts and Engineering II — Clusters 3 and 10. Traditional, northern, industrial and inner-city Britain are well represented: of these clusters, only the small group of three Welsh Mining Towns is missing.

The NCDS analysis was based on children in families with two parent figures, speaking English at home, and attending schools maintained by the local education authorities. It excluded children in the care of the local authorities and children with a father in the armed forces. The purpose of these exclusions was to ensure comparability of children between one local education authority and another, and comparability between evidence about attainment and evidence about the authorities' inputs into their local schools. This left 10,452 children potentially available for the study. Of these, 4,345 were living in the clusters and full information was available about them. The characteristics and attainment of these children were remarkably close to those of the whole national cohort: although we shall be drawing conclusions from less than a third of its total, that has produced no discernible bias.

The NCDS analysis differs from ours in one other small way: its social class groupings divide the population into six classes, based on the Registrar General's classifications, as follows:

1. Higher professional;
2. Other professional, managerial and technical;
3. III Non-manual (the more routine white collar jobs);
4. III Manual (supervisory and skilled);
5. Semi-skilled; and
6. Unskilled.

Differences in Attainment

After these methodological preliminaries we can turn to the questions we want to ask. First, does attainment vary among clusters? Tables 11.1 and 11.2 show that it does: the left-hand columns in each table present the actual deviations from the overall average attainments of eleven-year-old children in reading and mathematics. The differences are highly significant, statistically speaking: there is less than one possibility in a thousand that they could have arisen by chance.

Could these differences arise from variations in the resources provided by the local education authorities? Those variations are not trivial. Figures assembled by the Institute of Municipal Treasurers and Accountants (now the Chartered Institute of Public Finance and Accountancy) and the Scottish Education Department show total expenditure per pupil by regions ranging in 1968-69 from £105 and £108 in the North West and North Midlands to £126 and £183 in Wales and Scotland. Expenditure per pupil on salaries alone ranged from £66 and £67 to £83 and £90 in these four regions. Variations among local education authorities are larger still. Fifteen area-based factors, listed in Appendix IV, were selected for an exhaustive analysis of the resources invested in education and their effect on attainment. Of these, only two were related to attainment in a sufficiently significant and regular (that is to say linear) way to merit further study: they were the product of a penny rate (a measure of local wealth, which was positively related to attainment) and the number of primary pupils per 1,000 population (a measure, principally, of the prevalence of large families, which was negatively related to attainment). But when the influence of other factors, such as the social background of the children, was examined, these measures of educational inputs were found to throw no further light on the 'outputs' we were studying.

It does not follow that the quality of teaching and schools is irrelevant or could with impunity be cut down. The Bureau's authors give many reasons why their analysis, though based on the best data then

Table 11.1. *Comparison of Average Reading Ages of Children in*
NCDS Clusters, with and without Adjustment for Child-based Factors
(deviation in years from overall average)

NCDS Clusters	Unadjusted Score	Adjusted Score
1. London	0.19	-0.19
2. Regional Service Centres	-0.14	-0.12
3. Resorts	0.92	0.37
8. Engineering I	0.39	0.20
9. Textile Towns	-0.41	-0.39
10. Engineering II	0.40	0.36
11. Heavy Engineering and Coal	-0.52	-0.23
12. Inner Conurbations	-0.34	-0.16
13. Central Scotland	-0.49	0.16
χ^2 values	67.7	26.4

(SOURCE: National Child Development Study.)

The figures in this table are the fitted constants from the analyses of variance.
The additional statistics for these analyses are as follows (with adjusted analyses
in brackets): Overall Constant = 11.03 (11.19); Residual Mean Square = 7.5165
(5.7822); Total Variance = 7.6325; Degrees of Freedom = 8; Sample Size = 3867.

Table 11.2. *Comparison of Average Mathematical Attainments of*
Children in NCDS Clusters, with and without Adjustment for
Child-based Factors
(deviation in years from overall average)

NCDS Clusters	Unadjusted Score	Adjusted Score
1. London	0.03	-0.22
2. Regional Service Centres	-0.18	-0.17
3. Resorts	0.71	0.25
8. Engineering I	0.41	0.26
9. Textile Towns	-0.34	-0.39
10. Engineering II	0.26	0.21
11. Heavy Engineering & Coal	-0.42	-0.15
12. Inner Conurbations	-0.32	-0.20
13. Central Scotland	-0.15	0.41
χ^2 values	60.1	43.6

(SOURCE: National Child Development Study)

Overall Constant = 11.05 (11.11); Residual Mean Square = 5.0299 (3.9245);
Total Variance = 5.0977; Degrees of Freedom = 8; Sample Size = 3866.

available, is by no means the end of the story. Expenditure per pupil will tend to be highest where classes are small — for example, in sparsely populated rural areas and in inner cities where the numbers of children are falling — but there is no reason why attainment should be correspondingly higher there. To such calculations we would add the comment that it is worth trying to ensure that the long and formative years we all spend in schools (and the even longer years which teachers spend in schools) are a constructive and happy experience — even if that does not pay off in greater proficiency in reading and mathematics. Nevertheless, to discover among children who have been in school for at least six years, *no* meaningful association between the data which local education authorities assemble to help them plan their own services and two of the most crucial measures of the achievements of those services poses startling questions, some of which we return to later in this chapter.

Next we consider the child-based factors — all the social information the NCDS was able to assemble about children, their families and homes. Of these variables 20, listed in Appendix V, were eventually included in this study. The factors most strongly associated with attainment were the occupation of the father, the size of the family, the tenure of their housing (in particular was it a council house or owner-occupied?), low income (the child receiving free school meals or the family living on supplementary benefit), the child's use of a public library and parent-initiated contacts with the school. All are at least partly a reflection of the distribution of status, wealth or knowledge.

Are differences in cluster scores due to the differing social character and environment of the children in each cluster? Or does the general character of the towns themselves exert some additional influence? When the cluster scores are adjusted to take account of the assumption that these 20 factors will be related locally to educational attainment in the same way that they are related nationally, the differences between scores are greatly reduced and their rank orders change. These figures appear in the right-hand columns of Tables 11.1 and 11.2. They show, for example, that London, where the actual, unadjusted attainment of eleven-year-olds was more than two months ahead of the national average for reading and roughly equivalent to the average for mathematics, was doing less well by more than two months for both reading and mathematics than it would be expected to do when the influence of child-based factors is taken into account.

But Glasgow and Dundee — the two towns in the NCDS Central Scotland cluster — make a striking improvement: although their unadjusted scores are below the national average (well below for reading) their children do better (much better for mathematics) that would be expected when account is taken of the many social handicaps they suffer. This finding must be treated with caution. Most of the statistical improvement in these Scottish scores was achieved when account was taken of the influence of two variables — the tenure of housing (essentially the proportion of children in council housing) and parent-initiated contacts with schools. In Glasgow and Dundee 75 per cent of the eleven-year-old children in the NCDS sample lived in council housing; in all county boroughs the figure was only 45 per cent. In Glasgow and Dundee only 14 per cent of the children lived in owner-occupied housing, whereas for all county boroughs the figure was 44 per cent. To be a council tenant in a city where the great majority of people live in council housing, or an owner-occupier where very few people buy their own homes, may have meanings and influences which differ from those found in other cities. In Glasgow and Dundee both parents initiated contacts with the school for only 3 per cent of the children: in all county boroughs the figure was 22 per cent. Here too there are cultural differences. Glasgow parents do not easily approach teachers. Another puzzling feature of these figures is that the adjusted scores for reading and mathematics differ much more in the Scottish towns than in other clusters. For these reasons we shall not lay great weight on the Scottish evidence.

Apart from these findings which are difficult to interpret, the main conclusions we draw from these two tables are that Clusters 3, 8 and 10 — the Resorts and Engineering I and II — do best both in reality and when account is taken of the handicaps and advantages to which their children are exposed. Clusters 9, 11 and 12 — the Textile and Heavy Engineering Towns and the Inner Conurbations — do worst, both in reality and when account is taken of child-based factors. Although differences among the adjusted scores are much smaller than those among the raw, unadjusted figures, they are still statistically significant — dramatically so, for they could have arisen by chance in less than one in a thousand cases both for reading and for mathematics. These differences are significant in simpler common-sense terms too. When account is taken of their social handicaps and advantages, the children in the 'best' clusters are still nearly five months ahead of the average in reading and mathematics, and the children in the 'worst' clusters are still nearly five months behind the average. They are nearly ten months apart.

If we put aside the two Scottish towns, the clusters where children tend to do best are the 'newer' and more rapidly expanding towns. This suggests the missing clusters — the Residential and New Industrial Suburbs and the New Towns — would be doing better still. The worst performers are the clusters most typical of 'old', industrial and inner-city Britain. The relatively high attainment of the Engineering II cluster is also striking — particularly in reading.

Having established that there are factors at work in these clusters which produce important differences in attainment, we must next ask which of the child-based variables has this effect. Long years of research on the NCDS have produced a lot of information about the factors which influence educational standards. At this stage of their analysis the Bureau's authors examined the influence within each cluster of father's occupation, family size, housing tenure, income level, use of public libraries and parent-initiated contact with schools — all good discriminators between children in earlier, national analyses — to see if any of them were operating in unusual ways in particular clusters. They found that none of these factors were related in unusual ways to scores for reading. Only one showed an unusual pattern for mathematics.

Table 11.3 presents these rather confusing patterns. It shows mathematical attainment in each occupational group and cluster, when the influence of other factors is discounted. All the scores are measured, as before, as deviations in years from the national mean. As usual, the high scores generally appear in the higher occupational groups and in the Resorts, but there are exceptions to this rule. All three clusters of Engineering towns do well — particularly Engineering II — and they do particularly well in the middle and lower reaches of their social structure, among the children of routine non-manual workers and manual workers. In the Resorts, by contrast, the children of routine non-manual workers do less well than similar children in several other clusters (perhaps because these towns, depending heavily on service industries employing many such workers, have dipped into lower strata of ability to find them?). These results are statistically significant: there is less than a one per cent possibility that the differences they reveal could have arisen by chance. They suggest that the children of routine non-manual workers and manual workers have some advantages in mathematics (but not in reading) in engineering towns. That may not seem a particularly surprising result.

Thus a massive analysis shows only that the performance of children differs significantly from cluster to cluster, but, with this rather unsurprising exception, none of the usually revealing factors explain why. We conclude with some alternative hypotheses — and they are no more than hypotheses — which suggest where explanations may be sought.

Education: Cause or Effect?

It may be that, for children in general, educational attainment of the more readily measurable kinds is achieved through work motivated by the hope of success. Aspiration is important. Children, like other people, can survive great hardships but they cannot readily tolerate failure. Indeed, the abler among them turn most quickly from activities which seem likely to prove disappointing to others which promise to be more rewarding. They conceive of success and failure, we suggest, in educational terms (the approval of teachers, passing examinations, etc.) in career terms (getting good jobs, high pay, etc.) and in broader social and psychological terms (gaining friends, the approval of parents and neighbours, a sense of self-respect, etc.). These motives tend to reinforce each other, positively or negatively, to form a general level of aspiration which influences performance in school and elsewhere.

Thus, particularly for manual workers and the more routine non-manual workers who usually go to school and find work in and around their home towns, the drive for educational success will depend partly on the general character of those towns. Children, their friends, parents and teachers, will combine to form shared views about the prospects for achieving success through educational attainment. If opportunities for work — particularly the kinds of work which call for middle-grade qualifications of the sort attainable by large numbers of people — appear to be growing, then aspirations will rise and more children will do better at school. They have something to work for. If those opportunities are enlarged and sustained by matching opportunities of other kinds — for better housing, desirable consumer goods, nicer holidays, and so on — and these things too seem to be growing more attainable, then the educational drive will be enhanced.

We explained on pages 138-9 that rates of growth cannot usefully be extracted from other aspects of urban development and examined separately because, fast or slow, a town's pattern of growth influences every other aspect of its character. Education may be another aspect of a town's development which is inextricably related to many other of its characteristics. Mobility, inward, outward and within the town, may be a third. Growth, mobility and educational aspirations may all be positively related.

Table 11.3. Analysis of Variance Showing Mathematical Attainment by Father's Occupation in NCDS Clusters

NCDS Clusters Father's Occupation	London	Regional Service Centres	Resorts	Engineering I	Textile Towns	Engineering II	Heavy Engineering and Coal	Inner Conurbations	Central Scotland
I and II Professional Technical and Managerial	0.88	1.51	2.07	1.45	0.71	0.92	0.54	0.65	1.14
III Non-manual	0.77	−0.34	0.49	0.77	0.25	1.18	0.97	0.41	0.19
III Manual	−0.69	−0.66	−0.37	−0.03	−0.90	−0.30	−0.70	−0.75	−0.43
IV and V Semi-skilled and Unskilled	−1.21	−1.44	−0.46	−1.13	−0.88	−0.86	−1.43	−1.26	−1.08

(SOURCE: National Child Development Study.)

Overall Constant = 11.32; Residual Mean Square = 4.4765;
Total Variance = 5.1482; Sample Size = 4343; χ^2 on 24 degrees of freedom = 43.4, $p < 0.01$.

It may be argued that even in the most depressed towns there are shortages of skilled workers. A recent official study of the Northern Region comments on 'the co-existence of high levels of unemployment and vacancies in all jobs and, with respect to vacancies, particularly among the more highly skilled jobs'.[3] If skilled jobs are available for qualified people, our hypotheses might be thought to imply that youngsters will acquire the necessary qualifications, particularly if the alternative is greater likelihood of unemployment. Why don't they?

If in forming their aspirations they rely on the advice and expectations (unspoken feelings often being the most influential[4]) of parents, teachers and other adults who inevitably know more about the past than the future, youngsters' expectations of education and the labour market may lag behind reality. They underestimate opportunities. Even in an economy growing as slowly as Britain's, that will lead to scarcities of skills, particularly in the newer and more rapidly growing industries. Such lags and scarcities may be even greater in underemployed and poverty-stricken communities than in more prosperous ones, if pessimism about the future is more widespread there, and people are more reluctant to take risks. They have reason to be reluctant: unless they are unusually confident about their future, economic insecurity may well make the children of manual workers more cautious about taking their education further and thereby missing immediate opportunities for work.

Our evidence suggests that the children of professional, managerial and technical workers are not greatly affected by influences operating at urban scale. Why not? They probably differ only in operating in larger markets for education and for labour. Their parents tend to move more often and move further than other people, they commute further to work, and the children more often seek education and training away from home. Because they are competing in regional and national markets, they will be less affected by local circumstances. But in other respects their behaviour may be motivated in the same ways — aided by the higher aspirations they acquire from parents, teachers, friends and neighbours and the greater opportunities to be found in the more prosperous parts of the country in which they tend to congregate. The fact that our theory does not fit the behaviour of middle class children is part of the evidence which supports it.

In a telling sentence Eric Midwinter summed up a feature of urban industrial societies which we have, in effect, been examining: 'You tell me the social class composition of a given county borough and I'll tell you, within a few per cent, how many of its children are in the sixth form and how many are in university.'[5] Too many people have assumed that the only conclusions to be drawn from that observation are that middle class children do best at school, and we must break down the doors which exclude working class children from similar educational opportunities.

But it is the children themselves who have to take the risks of going through the doors to educational opportunity, and they will not do that in large numbers unless they are convinced the results will be rewarding. Working class children who get what a previous generation thought of as a middle class education have generally used that to secure middle class jobs and the life style which goes with them. And why not? Prolonged education probably demands greater sacrifices of them in leaving family, losing friends and postponing material comforts than it demands of middle class children, and they are entitled to make sure of their reward.

Those who really want to enable children to take their education further than their parents did must first convince them and their elders that this will give them greater opportunities for skilled work and a rewarding life than their parents had. That will be easier in the growing, prosperous towns of the 'new' Britain — towns which also recruit and sustain larger proportions of middle class people. A town's educational attainment and its social composition may be more the effects than the causes of economic growth and urban development.

If these are indeed the influences which explain our findings it is sobering to reflect that they are to be seen among children of only eleven years old. Although they are still only half way through the minimum period of schooling this country permits them, they are already in the undertow of tides running much further out in the labour markets they will eventually enter. Studies of these children at age sixteen (for which the data are already available) and in their twenties will throw further light on these issues.

The implications of these conclusions for Britain and its educational policies are sombre. They may help to explain why this country's economy grows so slowly and why so many of our children leave school so early[6], while reversing some of the causal relationships usually thought to explain those observations.

12 Paths to Glory

Much of this book has been devoted to things which go wrong. But the central and successful parts of a society must be studied before its peripheral and problematic elements can be understood. In this chapter we look at three groups of people who reached the top of their professions and ask whether the places in which they worked played any part in their success. Although our evidence is thin, this longitudinal approach to urban studies is important. The chapter may at least encourage others to do more fully researched work of this kind.

The more highly qualified and affluent people have 'careers', not just 'jobs'. They work in specialised labour markets which often compel them to move from place to place for training and advancement. Their skills, incomes and other assets — particularly their relatively easy access to house purchase and its capital gains, and their capacity to meet the costs of long-distance commuting — enable them to move about more freely than others. They operate in a national — sometimes an international — labour market, not a local market of urban scale. That is probably why, as we showed in the last chapter, the educational attainment of their children is less affected by local circumstances than the attainment of children from working and lower-middle class families.

What opportunities these more successful people find in particular towns is not, by itself, a very interesting question, for the town in which they work today may be only a temporary resting place in a career that will take them to many other towns, none of which may be the places where they have their homes. We should instead be asking how they use the whole array of places the country offers them to live and work in, what contributions different parts of this urban society make to the careers of the successful and what contributions those careers make to different kinds of places. We cannot answer all those complex questions but they are the issues to which this chapter is addressed.

Sources and Methods

We chose local government as the source for an exploration of these issues because the work of local government has to be done all over the country in a fairly uniform way through a fairly uniform hierarchy, and the people who do it serve clearly defined areas and populations. To increase this uniformity we confined the study to England. We know who are supposed to be the 'top' people in these professions, and we can estimate on various assumptions what a random distribution of career routes would look like and how far actual routes diverge from those patterns. Other occupations would be equally interesting, but they are harder to work with. Hotel managers are presumably concentrated in resorts, mining engineers on coalfields, barristers in London and professors in university towns — for various reasons which tell us nothing new about these places, and still less about other places. It is also difficult to identify the populations these professions serve or to compete their career routes with theoretically random patterns.

We picked three local government services which are unlikely to compete directly with each other for influence: education, housing and social services. Local government professions work partly in competition with each other — town clerks competing with treasurers, architects thriving where planners are less dominant. Thus had we picked such potential competitors for our study the more successful careers in each profession might be found in different places for reasons connected with the structure of local government rather than the character of those places. We sought the help of the chief officers in these three services in the English local authorities, first explaining the purpose of our study to the relevant professional associations and seeking their approval of it — an endorsement for which we are very grateful. (We would have studied town planners too, but were unable after many attempts to gain any support from their Institute.) To get as high a response rate as possible from exceedingly busy people, much pestered by questionnaires, we kept our questions to a minimum. There were only two. After explaining the purpose of our inquiry we asked for a curriculum vitae, and added 'If one or more of these jobs had a particularly formative influence on your professional development or advancement, please note this and briefly explain why the job proved to be so important to you.'

We are grateful for the helpful responses given by the majority of those whom we approached. Table 12.1 summarises the response rate after one follow-up letter sent to those slow in replying. Most of the chief officers who replied not only sent the curriculum vitae for which we asked but also commented on particularly formative influences in their careers. We shall draw on these comments later, after examining the places through which they passed.

Table 12.1. Response to Our Questionnaire by Chief Officers

	Total number despatched	Unavoidable Non-responses*	Usable replies Number	% of total
Education	95	nil	70	74
Social services	107	1	81	76
Housing	331	2	221	67

*Recipient dead or post vacant.

In order to decide whether a particular authority appeared in the careers of the successful more or less often than would be expected on a random basis, we first had to define what a random expectation would be. We made the crude assumption that the size of an authority's staff would be proportional to the size of its population. Thus posts in an authority with, say, 2 per cent of Britain's population were 'expected' to provide 2 per cent of the jobs mentioned in the careers of chief officers. If it did so it was awarded a score of 1.0. Correspondingly a score of 1.50 would indicate that it appeared 50 per cent more often than its share of the British population would have led one to expect; a score of 0.50 would mean that it appeared half as often as would have been expected. (Appendix VI provides a fuller account of the methods used in this study.)

This is a very crude assumption for there are many factors influencing these figures besides the populations of the authorities concerned. For reasons explained in Appendix VI, we did not distinguish separate jobs held within one local authority unless the officer concerned had worked elsewhere between one job and the next. Thus an authority which makes a practice of advertising all its posts and recruiting outsiders will appear more often than another which promotes from within its own ranks. Studies in other fields suggest that turnover of staff is not related in a simple linear fashion to the size of organisations: large firms, promoting from within, often retain proportionately more of their workers than small ones, and large local authorities may do likewise. There is some evidence that in housing management the smallest authorities tend to do this too. Frequent appearance in the lists may indicate not that a place attracts people, but that it drives them away: our data cannot distinguish moves which were promotions from those which were not. An authority with a group of senior officials likely to stay in the same posts for many years, blocking promotion from below, may score high because it constantly compels abler people in its middle ranks to move on. Another, with no promotional blocks, may retain this kind of person and be mentioned less often for that reason. A few years later the situations of these two authorities may be reversed.

The social services departments were created in 1971 by an amalgamation of services hitherto provided by children's, welfare and health departments. As a result, three different routes for careers were abruptly combined into one. At this stage the children's officers tended to be promoted ahead of their colleagues from the other branches of the new service. Thus authorities which prior to this had had large children's departments will be mentioned more often than those with large health and welfare departments; but the next generation of chief officers may be drawn from different sources.

For all these reasons it is clear that we must be cautious about drawing conclusions from our evidence. Detailed comparison of the scores of individual authorities would be misleading. We present no league tables. Instead we must look for the broader *types* of places which appear in the lists, and compare them with other broad types which do not appear.

The Chief Officers

We begin by outlining the common characteristics of our three groups of chief officers. Most began their careers soon after the war, often after several years in the forces. They are, in general, the 'men of 1948'. (The same generation now heads the civil service and much of industry and commerce.) And they are nearly all *men*. This helps to explain the pattern of mobility. Careers, one senses, generally came first; families followed, from place to place. It was a woman who said, 'After leaving X (in 1952), all my posts enabled me to live in Y . . . my reasons being (a) long-standing family ties; (b) a strong preference for living in Greater Manchester, and (c) my membership, from 1961 to 1974, of Y Urban District Council. I have never applied for posts with a view to long-term career development. . . .' That was an unusual response. Women together accounted for only 8 per cent of the social services directors, 2 per cent of the education officers and 4 per cent of the housing managers.

Where They Came From

The number of relevant posts held by each group before attaining their present posts was broadly similar, averaging 3.5 per social services director, 4.0 per education officer, and 3.2 per housing manager. Not surprisingly, the authorities mentioned most often in the curricula vitae of all three groups are the largest in the country: London, Middlesex, Lancashire, Essex, the West Riding, Birmingham, Liverpool, Leeds. Every one of these was mentioned frequently for at least one of the three services. But those appearing most often in relation to their populations are different. They are shown in Tables 12.3, 12.4 and 12.5.

Tables 12.2 and 12.3 show, for education and social services directors, all the authorities appearing more than twice as often as their populations alone would have led us to expect, with the exception of London authorities which will be discussed later. Devon, Newcastle-upon-Tyne and Lincolnshire — a scattered and diverse trio — appear in both lists. Table 12.4, listing the 'top-scoring' housing authorities, is confined to those appearing more than four times as often as their populations would have led us to expect: since these are in the main smaller authorities — mainly urban districts and municipal boroughs — high scores are more easily generated. But the number (between 4 and 7) of 'mentions' which get authorities into each list is very similar for all three tables.

Counties in the southern half of Britain have produced more than their proportionate share of the 'top' people in education and the social services. Smaller towns of between 40,000 and 90,000 people have been the main producers of talent in housing, many of them centres of rapid development, planned and unplanned, around London. Most of the rest are in the North West.

Table 12.2. 'Top-Scoring' Education Authorities

	Total population, 1961 (thousands)	Number of previous posts held by chief education officers	Score
Southend	165	5	5.4
Lincolnshire	333	6	3.2
Shropshire	302	5	3.0
Wiltshire	430	7	2.9
Newcastle-upon-Tyne	267	4	2.7
East Sussex	375	5	2.4
Devon	530	7	2.4
Coventry	306	4	2.3
Cornwall	335	4	2.1

Table 12.3. *'Top-Scoring' Social Services Authorities*

	Total population, 1961 (thousands)	Number of previous posts held by social services directors	Score
Oxfordshire	206	5	4.4
Southampton	204	4	3.5
Devon	530	8	3.5
Newcastle-upon-Tyne	267	4	2.7
Lincolnshire	333	4	2.2
Nottinghamshire	593	7	2.1

London authorities attaining similar scores were Ealing and Wandsworth.

Table 12.4. *'Top-Scoring' Housing Authorities*

	Total population, 1961 (thousands)	Number of previous posts held by housing managers	Score
Banbury	21	4	17.1
Lancaster	49	6	8.8
Leamington Spa	43	5	8.4
Maidenhead	35	4	8.2
Accrington	41	4	7.0
Hemel Hempstead	56	5	6.4
Harlow	57	4	6.3
St. Albans	50	4	5.8
Burton-on-Trent	50	4	5.8
Reigate and Redhill	54	4	5.3
Slough	81	5	4.4
Rotherham	85	4	4.2
Rochdale	86	5	4.2
Carlisle	71	4	4.1

London authorities attaining similar scores were Southwark and Edmonton.

London had to be treated separately because the widespread boundary changes which occurred when its local government was reorganised in 1965 made it difficult to assess the scores of London authorities in any consistent way. If we consider all the authorities in the area which is now Greater London, their combined appearance in the lists is roughly what the population of the capital would lead us to expect, rather more for the Social Services and less for Education. If we add other posts which chief officers had held in London, including jobs in central government, commercial organisations, national charities, independent schools and other academic institutions, then London appears appreciably more often than its population alone would explain. But it should be added that many of the officers were probably living outside London when they were working there.

What They Learned on the Way

We show in Appendix VI the question we asked about posts which had played a particularly formative part in these careers. The evidence derived from this one open-ended and optional question, to which many did not reply, is much too impressionistic to justify statistical analysis. But the great majority of respondents had something to say, and much of it was very interesting. We will take the three groups in turn.

More than either of the other two groups the education officers stressed the training and inspiration they had gained at crucial stages of their careers from leading figures in their profession, particularly in their first administrative posts. When describing such an experience, one education officer said, 'The opportunity of beginning my career in educational administration under such an outstanding figure as Dr. A was the greatest piece of good fortune I have had . . . six successive Assistant Directors became Directors of Education without having been Deputies from the A "stable".' Another said of two of his chiefs, 'One looked for qualities of educational and human leadership in the CEO. In B and C there was scarcely any possibility of disappointment: both were men of ideas, the former inspired by deep humanity, the latter remarkable as a superbly efficient administrator. I . . . owe almost everything to these two men and not a great deal to the environment in which they worked except insofar as they were counties liberal and supportive of education.' There were many other comments of this kind, paying tribute to lots of different people. Rarely was the same 'guru' mentioned twice.

Like the last quotation, a few comments stressed the character of the authority and its elected members. One noted two influences: '(a) the standards, values and attitudes of distinguished former CEOs . . . were still potent factors . . .; (b) the Education Committee included figures of national reputation who have made outstanding contributions to the education service, e.g. Lady D and Dame E.' For many, contact with the Committee was a formative influence for the education it gave them in politics: one respondent said of a county often torn by political conflicts 'I learnt a great deal of the need for political awareness while remaining politically neutral.'

After leadership and other human influences, the challenges of growth, change and reform were the most frequently mentioned factors in these careers. One director said that his work, while still a teacher, as secretary of a local inter-professional group 'during a period in which the Authority's comprehensive plans were under consideration . . . made me appreciate that the reorganisation of secondary education would be one of the most dominant issues in education for many years to come. . . . Essentially, therefore, I came into administration in order to play a part in the reorganisation of secondary education.' Another said that a county in which he worked 'had much leeway to make up and was on the threshold of Town Expansion schemes under the Town Development Act. In fact, from 1961-71 the percentage increase in the population was the highest in the country.' One senses the transforming experience people get from such periods in their lives:

> The most demanding and interesting job was being Deputy Education Officer in Z when F was the CEO. This was a period of great change in the education service and as F was playing a significant role at both national and local level the work carried out in Z Education Department was of great significance in influencing national decisions which were of great local importance. It was possible to undertake this commitment as well as being responsible for the day to day administration of a quite large County Borough because of the excellent support one received from an able and very small team of senior professional colleagues. This period was important to me personally because it showed that I had the capacity to work at a rate which I could not possibly conceive unless I had been under such pressure in handling very important educational issues and having to meet both national and local deadlines.

In assessing the four posts in his career which had most influenced him, one of his colleagues aptly summed up the influences we have noted: '(a) because of its introduction to educational administration, and life and problems within a large city; (b) because of the insights it provided into the educational and social needs of the whole range of ability; (c) because of the leadership of an outstanding CEO; (d) because of the opportunities and challenges of a large and rapidly developing city'.

We will deal more briefly with the other two groups, stressing the points at which they differ from the education officers. Whereas the local education authorities and their administrators were well-established long before the period we are discussing, the social services departments were created in April 1971 when the children's and social welfare departments were abolished and their functions combined. The new departments also assumed some responsibilities previously assigned to the health and education services. Since then the service has grown rapidly, but it is much less uniform than the larger and longer established education service, and the needs it has to meet vary much more from place to palce.

Of the directors who replied to us, 49 per cent had gained most of their experience in children's departments — the youngest but most highly trained of the new service's constituent parts. Most of the rest — 31 per cent — came from the social welfare departments; 9 per cent came mainly from the probation service, 7 per cent from public health departments, and others from elsewhere or from a mixture of these sources. One, for example, had been successively a probation officer, a senior child care officer, a lecturer in social work and a Home Office inspector before becoming a director of social services.

Although the influence of leadership and the profession's 'gurus' was mentioned, it played a much smaller part in the explanatory comments of social services directors than in those of education directors. Social workers, as one director later commented, tend to reject authority, teachers to accept it. (Both may learn equally from the experience.) The character of the authority and its council had for some been very important. One had worked for 'a fine, progressive authority and I was fortunate to be there in the period of great expansion. . . . The City was very much affected both by its historical background, its desire to 'lead the West', the influence of the University, and a keen Labour Council which was deeply concerned about its less fortunate residents.'

Important, also, were opportunities for learning political skills, once basic professional confidence had been acquired. 'A very astute Chief Officer initiated me into the values, if not virtues, of pragmatism, and the tortuous ways of wending one's path through the local authority committee jungle (favourite saying "we are governed by men, and not angels!").

In a service in which training was less standard or widespread, opportunities for training and more general education were more often stressed as playing a formative part in people's careers. 'While employed by W, I had the opportunity of attending full-time at the London School of Economics . . .'. Opportunities for teaching were important too. One director said the foundations of his philosophy for his service were laid when 'the County Council agreed to release me to lecture on the Younghusband Course at the Nottingham Polytechnic, so that I could combine teaching with research and my normal departmental responsibilities.' Others deliberately moved into full-time teaching posts for a while.

Growth and reorganisation were again formative influences. 'I . . . found a Committee insisting on an immediate ten year programme for development — which eventually allowed the field force to increase from 3½ to 60 social workers and for the budget to treble.' Others presented a more sombre picture of situations calling for development against heavy odds — for example, in 'an authority with an appalling record and poor performance'. Another recalled a job that 'was the most demanding and most difficult. It was in every respect pioneering. . . .'

Although middle-sized authorities scored high in Table 12.3, comments on the size of the area and its services tended to favour the extremes. Some felt that small authorities had given them more responsibility early in their careers for a wider range of tasks; others felt that large ones provided more stimulating colleagues, and more opportunities for specialisation and for training within the service and on secondment.

The housing service is even more diverse in structure and character. Housing conditions, needs and programmes vary enormously. The authorities we are dealing with include some of the biggest landlords and developers in the world. The London County Council in its heyday had nearly a quarter of a million tenants and was building thousands of houses a year. In some cities these departments house over half the population. But other authorities have only a few thousand houses and are unlikely to build many more.

Unlike the other services we have considered, legislation does not oblige local housing authorities to appoint a committee or a chief officer, and there is no central body of inspectors. The chief officers of the service have various titles and come from a wide range of professional fields. Most of those who replied to us began as housing assistants, clerks or rent collectors in local housing authorities. Some were public health inspectors or clerks in their departments, and others came from various levels of the engineers', surveyors' or treasurers' departments. A few had worked for private landlords and housing associations. These patterns reflect the history of the local authorities' varying commitments to housing, which in some authorities is still only emerging from the other local departments and services among which its responsibilities have previously been divided.

Leaders were occasionally mentioned, but even less often by this group than by the social service directors. In a profession still searching for an independent identity it is perhaps less clear who the leaders are or what they should teach their followers. Opportunities for meeting people — tenants, applicants for council housing and others — were more often mentioned as a formative influence, perhaps because these men had at earlier stages of their careers been largely confined to paper work and impersonal technicalities. One recalled his first experience of 'day to day management of Council dwellings (rent collections, arrears, social welfare, transfers, exchanges, aged people's schemes, etc.). The final involvement with tenants is the end product of housing and experience gained in this position is invaluable.' Another 'changed to Housing Department in order to become involved with *people*'. Training was important: 'eventually realised at the age of 26 [said one manager] that it was a dead end job unless I took often repeated advice of the Housing Manager to study for Institute of Housing examination for professional qualification' — which is something he probably had to do through a correspondence course.

But the most distinctive theme in these replies was the progress being made over this period towards an increasingly 'comprehensive' service in which responsibilities previously scattered amongst other departments were brought together into one department as local authorities accepted that their housing functions were likely to constitute a continuing, major programme of work, not merely a temporary series of building and clearance projects. Hence managers stressed 'experience on . . . a very wide basis at senior level particularly involving the establishment of a comprehensive Housing Service and first Housing Advice Centre'. Another said 'I was . . . extremely fortunate in having a very pro-housing superior officer who insisted that as Housing Manager his views should not be secondary to that of the usual Chief Officers of that time, i.e., Treasurer, Town Clerk, Engineer and Surveyor.' Urban growth and the resulting growth of many housing departments were important because they provided opportunities of these kinds. Some new towns and major town expansion schemes became training schools, in effect, for housing managers and test beds for the development of a new kind of housing department. One manager said his experience in a rapidly developing new town was

> probably the greatest single impact on my career. I . . . became responsible, inter alia, for repairs and maintenance; after a few weeks I had to take over a new maintenance depot, staff and stock it, and generally to become much more involved in technical matters than hitherto. Several of the housing contracts in "my" area comprised technical innovation with the resultant frequent and new problems. This opened up new dimensions on the development of my career — the angry tenants, the protest marches, the petitions and rent strikes on the one hand with the

frequent heated arguments and discussions with the architects, consultants and contractors on the other. Three years purgatory — most exhilerating and I would not have missed it for the world.

Conclusions

We asked two questions of 372 people. Although they are different, the three local government professions to which they belong will to many seem very similar occupations. Town planners might have been different, and the many occupations in industry and commerce even more so. Our conclusions must be cautious, but we believe we have at least shown that more extensive research of this kind would be worth doing.

We are dealing with the selection and training of élites. People who become responsible for the expenditure of millions of pounds, the welfare of thousands of people and the employment of hundreds of staff have first to gain confidence in their own technical skills. They must be able to recognise the contributions of different professions within a service and make constructive use of them, to understand the part which their own service can play along with others on a wider stage, and to work with those who have the essentially political function of managing and arbitrating between these conflicting interests. Where are they likely to gain those capacities for operating on successively larger stages and the approbation of those who select people for successively more senior posts?

When the holder of one of the top posts in any field retires, the man who fills that vacancy leaves another to be filled by someone else — and so on down the hierarchy, the vacancy moving in the opposite direction to the promotions till it eventually 'hits the ground' in the form of a post taken by a new recruit to the occupation who leaves no vacancy (except at school, on a training course or in another occupation). The units in the field which are growing fastest and attracting the largest numbers of new recruits will therefore have a better chance than others of providing the initial starting point for careers, successful or unsuccessful.

To succeed, the recruits must find opportunities for learning their jobs, and for gaining the attention of those who promote people. Innovation, organisational development and growth in the scale of a community and the services it needs will make some places more fruitful training grounds from both points of view.

In a well-established field like educational administration, the leading spirits will play important parts in training and selecting the élite who eventually succeed them. A famous chief education officer, recently retired, illustrated the process in a comment he made on a first draft of this chapter, 'I always looked at the nature of the job I wanted done in my office and then looked carefully at the folk who came from offices where the CEO was noted for qualities I was looking for. . . . There was a time when if a CEO wanted 'an administrator' he would look at the North Riding — if he wanted someone who was steeped in classroom progress and the physical impact of buildings he would turn to Leicestershire — if he wanted as much of both as he could get he would look to Hertfordshire or Bristol.'

This rephrases the question rather than answers it. If winners are picked from the best training stables, then where do the leading trainers go? Our evidence suggest they go to nice places — prosperous, growing, southern counties and middle-sized towns not too far from London and Birmingham. Other studies have shown that the same places often stand high among the preferences people express when they are asked where they would ideally like to live.[1] This finding is particularly striking in the case of the social services directors, who came from the prosperous and leafy counties to take charge of work which is most needed and most heavily staffed in the least salubrious parts of the country.

Public intervention helps to create those patterns — and can change them. The social services directors often came from places with active children's committees and large children's departments. The experience of housing managers shows that the more comfortable counties and suburbs need not be the only places to which ambitious people steer. Being concerned mainly with the building and management of public housing, they often gained their spurs in places where there were large public housing programmes — in new and expanding towns, growing industrial centres and the smaller northern boroughs with major re-development schemes.

Two past presidents of the Association of Directors of Social Services explained some of the advantages of the more prosperous, middle-sized counties when they were commenting on a first draft of this chapter. One said, 'Counties with populations between 350,000 and 500,000 seem to provide senior jobs with most satisfaction . . . below 200,000 there never seemed to be enough money available to pay for the management structure which was needed — it was not possible, for example, to fund adequately either a training officer or a research officer. With populations around one million, it was difficult for senior staff to feel they had a complete grasp of all that was going on.' The other said that the shire counties enabled senior officers to 'get on with the job' more freely by delegating more to them, partly because their geography compelled them to do so, partly because Conservative councillors were more willing to delegate than Labour councillors.

The two Directors may in effect be repeating a point we have already made. Whatever their political colour, attractive, expanding, buoyant places are most likely to attract competent, ambitious, innovative people, to whom powers are more likely to be delegated. This is the point at which our findings must be related to those of the previous chapter. If we consider these people and their more successful colleagues in many other occupations not only as young professionals and executives but as parents of the next generation, and as rate-payers, voters and school managers, it is easier to understand why the children in such prosperous, developing places are likely to perform rather better than similar children in more depressed places. The child-based factors we examined in that chapter – factors such as family size, housing tenure and contact with schools and libraries – capture some of these influences but by no means all of them.

Big cities do also appear in the careers of the successful. London, as the nation's capital, attracts many people to it at some stage in their careers (but not necessarily to its local government). Newcastle-upon-Tyne and Southampton may operate as regional capitals. But the only other sizable city to score highly is Coventry – one of the 'middle England' towns of our Engineering II cluster with a reputation for innovation in many fields. (Slough, another town in that cluster, also appears.)

The centres of deprivation and social conflict – the big, old industrial cities of the North and the less buoyant parts of the West Midlands – have not attracted or created a large share of the future leaders of public services to which we look for effective programmes to meet the needs of such cities. Those patterns can be changed. In an attempt to bring about such changes many education authorities have tried in recent years to recruit more and better staff to teach in priority area schools and have paid them more for doing so. But unless policies of this kind are adopted on a wider scale the paths to glory will not pass through England's more sombre urban scenes, or give our leaders first-hand experience of this country's most intractable urban problems.

Part III

13 Conclusions

We describe this final chapter as Part III to distinguish it from the evidence and analyses presented in Part II. Here we summarise only the main findings presented in Part II before resuming the discussion of questions posed in Part I; we will draw on earlier chapters but not confine ourselves to points which can be derived directly from them. We are not offering authoritative research findings; rather this is the conclusion of an essay into which a good deal of research has been woven. Some of our assertions are firmly rooted in the evidence of previous chapters, and some are more speculative: we distinguish one from the other by noting the chapter or pages when evidence has been presented earlier in the book.

The Central Questions

What kinds of city and what patterns of urban development will provide better opportunities and living conditions for manual workers in general, and for the most vulnerable people in particular? Will the same cities provide a more equal distribution of living conditions among different social groups and classes, or are different patterns of development required for greater equality? If the history and character of a city play a part in shaping the level and distribution of living standards among its citizens, can we by deliberate policies and programmes change cities in chosen ways? What kinds of policies, pursued through what instruments, and at what geographical scales, are likely to achieve this? If such policies succeed, will they increase the number of 'good' cities in Britain, or will they merely shift them around the map? Will solutions at an urban scale of action help to resolve or only to redistribute the problems perceived at larger scales of action?

These were the central questions to which we were led by the debate about urban policies recounted in Part I. They are much too complicated to answer in a complete and authoritative fashion. But they are worth exploring, even in tentative ways, in order to clarify the aims and potentialities of urban policies and to pose the more limited questions to which precise answers can in time be given. We try to do that in this chapter by looking first at national trends in the economy and next at patterns of urban development. These pages lead us to a cautious but not completely defeatist conclusion about the scope for urban planning. We then turn to consider what can be done by planners and others concerned with towns and their public services. Finally we consider the implications of our findings for research workers and for a wider public.

The National Context[1]

In Britain, as in other countries, productivity is advancing across a wide range of industries and the numbers of workers required to produce a given output of goods continues to fall. Although world demand for these goods is rising, there are signs that more and more of the growth in industrial production will take place in the more rapidly developing economies of the third world. Britain is a relatively rich country which has been slow to reorganise and re-equip its industries, partly because it was protected until recently by its imperial markets and preferences. The reorganisation which belatedly gathered speed in the late 1960s will go much further. To attract and retain the capital they need to survive, many of our older industries must transform their productive equipment and drastically reduce their labour forces, or find other ways of cutting their wage bills.

The massive reduction in jobs already brought about for these reasons has been roughly counterbalanced in numbers by the growth of new jobs, particularly in service industries and white collar work in both the public and private sectors of the economy. The supply of labour adapted remarkably well to these changes in demand through the recruitment of new workers to expanding industries and through early retirement and prolonged schooling, which took many workers out of the labour force or postponed their entry to it. But changes in demand have moved too fast to be wholly accommodated in this way. Moreover the growth in jobs has been mainly for women and for workers with the more routine white collar skills, while the jobs lost have been mainly for men and for skilled and semi-skilled manual workers. One kind of worker cannot readily substitute for the other. In addition growth and decline usually occur in different places. Meanwhile the supply of labour has increased as more and more women enter the labour force, and (more temporarily) as the numbers of school leavers continue to rise. These are the main trends now working on a national scale to increase unemployment, particularly among manual and the youngest workers, both of whom were those already most likely to be out of work.

Patterns of Urban Development[2]

Each town has its own history and its own pattern of growth. It grew rapidly at particular periods of time, and attracted and developed particular kinds of industry and particular kinds of workers. Each can be grouped into a category or cluster with a distinctive industrial base, creating through its labour market a distinctive economic and social structure. The general level and distribution of living standards among its people — particularly its working class people who, being less mobile, are more confined to the local labour market — depends on the history of the towns, the industries assembled there and the impact made upon them by developments in the national economy.

Some clusters of towns are more sharply distinguished from each other than the rest: London, the cities in the centres of the old conurbations, and the towns of central Scotland, which are all declining in population, and the residential and new industrial suburbs, the new towns and the resorts, which are all growing. They are in a sense opposite sides of the same coin, for over the years the selective migration of people from the inner parts of the biggest cities and the declining industrial centres to the leafy suburbs, new towns and resorts has shaped the contrasting characters of each.

But the other clusters, accounting for about two-thirds of British towns, are less clearly distinguished — at least by the variables which most interest us. They are predominantly industrial, working class towns, some depending on older, less prosperous industries, others on newer, more prosperous ones. They represent much of urban Britain ranging, in the folklore of television, from old-fashioned *Coronation Street* to affluent *Crossroads*.

All social groups and classes tend to benefit from the prosperity of the growing towns which depend more heavily on service industries, public and private, and the newer forms of manufacturing, but it is the manual workers in general and the least skilled in particular who benefit most — to judge from their likelihood of getting a job, owning a car and travelling to work in one, and also from the educational attainments of their children (see Chapter 11) and the general standards of housing in these towns. There is some evidence that other potentially vulnerable groups, such as lone parents bringing up young children and women workers in general, also do better in these more prosperous places (see pages 113-14).

The growing, prosperous city, the city which is kindest to its more vulnerable citizens and the city which distributes its opportunities more equally than most can all be the same place. At urban scale at least, we do not have to choose between progress and equality. That may be due partly to differential mobility — to the fact that the more highly qualified and more highly paid people operate in a national labour market, while the less skilled and lower paid tend to be more confined to local labour markets. The former move house more often, move further, and travel longer distances to work than the latter. Thus they compete with more people of their own kind for the expanding opportunities in more prosperous towns, while the less skilled, being less mobile, gain more from a town's prosperity and suffer more from its poverty. But that is not the main reason why prosperity and equality (only slightly greater equality it should be remembered) tend to go together. If it were, other relatively immobile groups (women by comparison with men, and teenage and elderly workers by comparison with workers of 'prime age', for example) would also benefit relatively more from general prosperity and suffer relatively more from the lack of it. But they do not. In comparison with people of their own kind elsewhere, workers in the prime of life suffer more than teenage workers, and men suffer more than women from the high unemployment rates of depressed urban economies (see Chapter 9).

The primary causes of these patterns are to be found in the economic structure of different kinds of town. The industries of the more depressed towns rely more heavily on skilled and semi-skilled men doing manual jobs, and these are the men who have lost ground as those industries have declined. The more skilled workers among them are rarely unemployed for long: it is the opportunities for promotion and higher earnings which they are likely to lose. But in taking less skilled work than they would get elsewhere, they push unskilled men out of the bottom of the labour market into unemployment. The relative immobility of the unskilled is thus a secondary cause of their deprivations because it prevents them from gaining access to growing industries, some of which rely fairly heavily on semi-skilled and unskilled labour in the more prosperous towns.

Prosperity, mobility, full employment and equality are all connected with growth. But we must beware of relying too heavily on growth as the explanatory variable to be used. It is not every pattern of growth which has benign effects: the seaside resorts, for example, are among the most rapidly growing towns but they have unemployment rates somewhat above average. Nor is it every pattern of decline which has disastrous or unequalising effects: London's population is declining faster than that of almost any other city, yet it is behaving in many ways as growing towns do.

Moreover a town's growth cannot be extricated from other characteristics and its influence understood in isolation from them. Demographic growth is closely related to a town's industrial base and its economic and social structure, its inward and outward rates of migration (see page 116), its marriage rates, (see page 137), the character of its housing (see pages 86-7) and probably to the educational aspirations and attainments of its children (see Chapter 11). High growth rates usually (but not always) go with new and more prosperous manufacturing and service industries employing a high proportion of non-manual workers with high rates of inward and outward migration. These towns have a relatively young population of whom large proportions are married by the time they reach their thirties and forties. They have generally good housing conditions and high rates of car ownership. It is not growth alone but many interrelated factors which constitute a more prosperous and a significantly (but not dramatically) more equal society.

Prosperous working-class towns, such as the cluster discussed in Chapter 10, probably have three important characteristics which we have not been able to measure. They appear to demand a lot of middle-range skills for which middle-range incomes are paid. They may have fewer gaps or discontinuities in their ladders of opportunity — fewer points in the hierarchies of jobs, incomes, housing and educational opportunities at which a move to the next rung becomes very difficult. The different sectors of the urban economy appear to be in closer equilibrium with each other: middle range incomes are matched by middle-price housing, and by an education system equipped to give people the middle range skills they need in such an economy. There are fewer disjunctions between the 'markets' operating in these different sectors of the urban economy. Over many years, the general and reasonably well balanced expansion of opportunities in such towns may have reduced the risks taken by those who move to new jobs, new houses and neighbourhoods, and by those who take their education further than was customary for members of their family or class. If so, that may increase their motivation to succeed, and hence the general level of attainment. New towns and the newer industrial suburbs (for which we were unable to get educational data) may share these characteristics. We cannot prove these generalisations: all we can say is that the evidence available to us seems to fit reasonably comfortably with them.[3]

We do not conclude that attempts to achieve better conditions for deprived people and to create a more equal society must wait until economic development enables a city to move 'naturally' in these directions — slums being left undisturbed until the city's industrial structure generates sufficient earnings to pay for better housing, disease being left untreated until growing prosperity creates a more healthy environment, and no attempt being made to improve educational standards until local industry makes matching demands for more highly trained labour. But our conclusions do suggest that progress on these fronts will indeed be more costly, demanding larger subsidies for housing (or transport or both) and heavier expenditure on health care, education and other services than would be required to achieve similar progress in more prosperous cities.

Social programmes of this kind may also impose higher social costs on deprived people in depressed towns. Re-housing in council estates on the fringes of Glasgow may have been achieved at the cost of higher transport charges and reduced job opportunities for the tenants.[4] Likewise higher educational attainment in a town offering few opportunities for better qualified people may be achieved at the cost of under-employment or outward migration for the young people concerned. For example, Welsh educational attainment is generally high, but the qualifications of those who stay in the Welsh valleys are low (see page 94). The National Child Development Study shows that for the children of manual workers and the less skilled non-manual workers the general expansion of a city's economy is more closely associated with educational attainment at the age of eleven than any input made by the local education authorities which we have yet been able to measure. The growth of a city and the prosperity of its economy seem to have no influence on the educational attainment of the children of the more mobile professional and managerial workers. Because their aspirations are less likely to be bounded by the local labour market, this tends to support our general conclusions (see Chapter 11).

The 'polity' of a town may be as important as its economy; indeed the two cannot be clearly distinguished, for each influences the other. The scale and the innovative capacity of its public services, the vigour of local leadership, the accessibility of the political system to newcomers, and its responsiveness to the demands and needs of deprived minorities: all these play important parts in shaping the status and living conditions of the less skilled and more vulnerable social groups. The public authorities in an expanding, mobile and generally hopeful community are likely to find it rather easier to act with generosity and foresight than are those in more deprived places. But we can offer little more than consistent speculation on these important points (see page 142).

What Can We Do?

Outside the new towns and other major expansion schemes, town planners' powers have been mainly of a negative kind. They can grant or refuse permission to develop and thus steer developers away from some sites and towards others. They can exact benefits for the community in return for permission to develop on sites which attract developers. But if no-one wants to develop at all, there is little that planners can do. At the best of times it is only the minority of 'footloose' industry which is willing to move and can be transferred from one town to another. The Inner Urban Areas Act is one of the measures now beginning to give local authorities more positive powers — but only in a few inner city areas and only on a small scale.

Nevertheless it is possible to create growing, prosperous towns with many good features. The new towns — some of them situated in relatively depressed regions of the economy (page 190) — have demonstrated this. It is also possible to take a whole sector of the urban economy and by massive investment over many years transform the quality of the living conditions it provides and ensure that a wider range of people gain more equal access to these benefits: council building and slum clearance programmes have together achieved this in Britain (see pages 86-7). Local histories and case studies show that towns on the brink of decline can be 'rescued' and turned into more prosperous and probably more equal places: Swindon is an example (see pages 140-41). To make a success of such projects calls for hard labour, political flair and commitment, and a great deal of public and private investment. They were 'planned' in the sense that they did not come about accidentally or easily. But the crucial human contributions to the achievement were political and administrative, owing little to the skills taught in the town planning schools. From our evidence, however, we cannot say whether the cost of these schemes was acceptable, or whether the same results could have been more economically achieved in some other community in other ways.

Economic failure and the unemployment it produces lie at the centre of this country's problems. Britain's high unemployment is not like a patch of bad weather, which struck the economy unexpectedly and will blow itself out before long. It is the predictable outcome of inadequate, ill-judged investment and of the long overdue attempt, encouraged and heavily financed by Governments, to reorganise and re-equip backward industries in an increasingly competitive world. For industries which cannot reorganise the only way of securing a return on capital regarded as adequate by the market is to rely on low paid, ill-organised labour. Investment governed only by the motives of the capital market will often succeed in driving labour costs down in one or other of these ways, often by closing uneconomic plants, in nationalised and private enterprises alike. But investment designed to use and develop the potentialities of the local labour force will also be needed if the more destructive effects of reorganisation are to be avoided. Because this cannot be the market's first priority, most of that investment must come from central or local authorities.

Some local authorities already do invest some of the large funds now available to them in local enterprises, but this is usually for special or rather accidental purposes, not part of a broader economic strategy for a town and its people.[5] The redundancies and closures which follow from reorganisation and rationalisation are heavily concentrated in particular kinds of town such as the inner conurbations and the towns of central Scotland. Investment designed to provide new jobs will be needed in the same areas. Fortunately our evidence suggests there is no reason why towns occupied by industry, which was once prosperous but now failing, should not again provide a base for prosperity: there is nothing inherently destructive about the towns themselves. Manufacturing should certainly make some contribution to their revival, but we must increasingly look to other industries if we are to gain much leverage on the economy. Over the country as a whole, manufacturing now accounts for only a third of the labour force and that proportion is likely to fall still further. Many now look to small scale enterprises and co-operatives to bring about revival. These may indeed play an important part, but it would be a mistake to rely too heavily upon them. As well as a few winners, there are many small enterprises which offer insecure jobs for low pay to ill-organised workers. The inner cities already have enough insecure, low-paid jobs.

More generally our research shows that we need a better understanding of the interaction among different sectors of a town's economy — its industries and labour market, its housing and education, its health and social services, and so on. Although society has divided them up for intellectual and administrative convenience, placing them in different academic disciplines and bureaucratic departments, we must never forget that we are talking abour the work, housing, education, health and social needs of the same people. How they behave in any one of these fields will depend on what is happening to them in the other fields.

The Government's recent White Paper on Policy for the Inner Cities shows that this lesson is being learned.[6] It lists in an Annex the contributions to programmes for the inner cities to be expected from services concerned with education, social services and health, besides those concerned with housing, transport, derelict land and other matters falling within the field of the Department of the Environment, the Ministry principally concerned. But the paragraphs of this Annex devoted to social services say nothing about helping poverty stricken families or lone parents to get training or jobs. Like most statements about social work, they deal with women, children and the elderly — people assumed to be outside the labour market. (Yet a recent report on social work with deprived families in an inner neighbourhood of Melbourne showed that when the bold decision was taken to hand over the management of the project to the families themselves — converting it from a social work agency to a 'self-managed community' — greater attention was given to jobs, money, education, welfare rights and political action. This change of emphasis also laid greater stress on the needs and concerns of the men within these families.[7])

The paragraphs in the White Paper devoted to education are confined almost entirely to children and their schools. Numerous books and articles produced in the past fifteen years follow the same pattern. The central criterion for educational policy in most of this literature has been the extension to working class children of opportunities for secondary and higher education hitherto confined to small elites. This is an important aim. But the aim of enabling men and women already working in manual jobs to acquire new skills and interests has attracted far less attention in research, in public expenditure and in educational policies. Yet this may now be even more important than the conventional objectives of education. Moreover, our evidence suggests that if educational programmes for people already in the labour force can help to create a more buoyant and hopeful urban economy, this may eventually exert as great an influence on the education of young children as anything the education authorities are doing in the schools (see Chapter 11). Economic and social development may be as much a cause as an effect of high educational attainment.

Those more directly concerned with urban and regional planning have also found it difficult to take account of the links between different sectors of the economy. Britain's main public investments in industry have often been designed either to prop up failing enterprises which employ large numbers of voters or to subsidise capital-intensive projects like aluminium smelters and oil refineries, without regard to the impact of either kind of investment on the general development of opportunities in the labour market and on other sectors of the economy. The gaps in each sector which most urgently need to be filled are not identified and the interactions between sectors are not well understood. Research in an underemployed area into which massive public investment had recently been poured showed that growth in the output of agriculture, government and professional services may do more to multiply employment and incomes than equivalent growth in engineering, hotels and heavy industry, which have generally been given higher priority for public investment. Investment in different industries creating jobs for different kinds of workers has widely varying repercussions on the rest of the community – repercussions which are too rarely taken into account.[8] These problems are too often neglected because those responsible can act – and hence may think – for only one sector of the economy at a time. The massive diversion of public expenditure from the building of new housing to the improvement of old houses which took place during the late 1960s switched real income on a large scale from poorer to richer and from older to young householders, without any public discussion of these foreseeable implications.[9] We have already quoted research suggesting that families moved to peripheral estates from inner city housing may end up, in cash terms, poorer than they began when account is taken of the earnings of wives and children as well as heads of households and the travel costs and periods of unemployment which all of them may experience as a result of re-housing.[10]

Planning permissions, which have often been given on terms prescribing conditions to be fulfilled by the developers, rarely include obligations to create jobs or training opportunities. What are called 'planning gains', secured from developers in return for permission to develop, usually consist of money payments, or small amounts of space for road widening, public housing or parks[11] – and the scope for this kind of local 'rake-off' must now be reduced by the development gains tax, introduced in the Finance Act of 1974, which obliges developers to pay a larger share of their gains to the national tax-payer through central government. Henceforth such bargains should more often be struck for the provision of, say, ten skilled and twenty semi-skilled jobs for people living in a specified town, with an offer of training if the relevant skills are not available locally.

To help local councillors and their officials to consult the public and co-ordinate their thinking about all these problems, some regular public statement of their plans for the longer term future of their area will be needed. The Layfield panel may have been right to reprimand the Greater London Council for trying to use the restricted powers and cumbrous procedures of a structure plan for this purpose, but only because those were the wrong instruments for the job. (See page 20). Every major local authority should be thinking as comprehensively as possible about the future of their area, and the impact which every development, inside and outside their area, may have upon those living within it. A strategic plan, outlining the authority's main objectives and showing how they are to be attained, should be prepared for the policy committee or 'cabinet' of the majority party in the council. Town planners, just like other professions, should contribute to this strategy, but they have no prescriptive right or monopoly in preparing it. It will call for the help of councillors and officials responsible for each of the main local services. Strategic planners will need procedures, less slow moving than those of structure planning, for informing and consulting different interests and for making themselves accountable to the public. It has been suggested that the transport policies and pro- grammes which deal with transport expenditure in each county, and the Scottish regional reports (first published in 1976) which are to provide a general review of trends and priorities for each Scottish region, may be more helpful models.[12] Both look ten to fifteen years ahead, and are to be 'rolled forward' regularly. Both may be published, but neither has to be. If each major authority had to produce, every year or two, a 'County Report' formulating general objectives, evaluating relevant economic and social trends, and showing how the strategic plans of the autho- rity's major services and of other neighbouring authorities are to be reconciled, that would cover a wider field than a structure plan and permit a quicker response to unforeseen developments. If these County Reports were published regularly and submitted to the central govern- ment's regional authorities, they could eventually supplant structure plans as the strategic planning document requiring formal approval from the secretary of state.

Many of the things we have commended in this book — high levels of employment, greater equality in the distribution of opportunities, good housing, plenty of part-time jobs for married women and high educational attainments — are loosely associated with development and growth. Because the economy is faltering and the increase in this country's population is, in the short run, more or less fixed at about zero, that may suggest that urban planning is a 'zero sum game', any gain secured by one town being achieved at the cost of equivalent losses elsewhere.

This must be at least partly true. But it would be absurd to assume that the planning game has to be exactly 'zero sum'. It might, after all, be worse. No one would argue that mismanagement which made things deteriorate in, say, Glasgow must necessarily improve things elsewhere. And if the planning game could turn out worse than zero sum, it could also turn out better. Many of the things we have commended are easier to achieve in a buoyant economy, but they are not directly tied to rates of demographic or economic growth. Innovation, development, education, mobility — as well as humanity, fairness and hope — these are among the crucial characteristics we are looking for, not a mere increase in numbers. It is in fact misleading to think in terms of a contrast between cities which gain and cities which lose people and wealth: the growing cities recruit *and* lose more people, proportionately, than the declining ones, and people within them probably change their jobs more often.[13] Thus the most important distinction may be between places with high and low rates of *activity*. Moreover, to assert that the sum total of 'good' cities cannot be increased until the national economy has first generated more 'good' things to make that possible, is to assume that national development occurs on a different plane without being specifically located somewhere on the map. But solutions to national problems are in fact worked out on the ground, in cities, which may as they develop make a contribution to the nation's welfare as well as to their own.

Future Research

In many disciplines a growing amount of research is being done on what might be called 'urban studies', but much of it is less interesting than it should be. We believe we have shown that innovation, social change and economic growth must be taken seriously, both as policy aims and as research themes — not as an alternative to concern about social justice and redistribution of the fruits of growth, but partly because justice and redistribution are much harder to achieve without growth.

We have also shown that the best way to understand problems is to start by learning about success. We shall not understand who gets unemployed, and why, unless we first study the changing opportunities open to those in work. To understand poor educational attainment we must first learn about high attainment. Our general plea is for a better understanding of the growth and evolution of urban settlements, the links between one type of settlement and another within a wider urban society, and the forces which shape the distribution of their benefits and costs among different kinds of people.

To explore these questions calls for a better understanding of three main aspects of urban society. The first of these might be described as the sources of, and the motives for, investment in towns, industries and their day to day management.[14] Unless we constantly ask 'who builds, develops and governs; and why?', we shall not understand the scope and limits of present institutions and programmes or appreciate why every definition of a social problem or its solution should trigger in our minds the further questions: 'A problem for whom?' 'A solution for whom?' 'Whose city is this?'

Second, we need a better understanding of the links and interactions between the different sectors of an urban economy — its markets for labour, housing, education, health care, recreation and much else. Each sector is closely connected with the others because it provides insights about the same people behaving as workers, householders, students, and so on.

Third, we need a better understanding of the relations and interactions between the different spatial scales of urban settlement, and the way in which patterns and developments at one scale — that of the urban neighbourhood, the city, the region, the nation, a continent or the world — may be related to patterns and developments at other scales. What at one scale appears to be a solution may at others turn out to be a problem. This study has concentrated mainly on the urban scale, but it has repeatedly had to pose (and failed convincingly to answer) questions about other scales of settlement.

If we turn from major research themes to approaches and methods, it is clear that we need historical, longitudinal studies of the evolution of settlements and their people, as well as the static data which constitutes the bulk of our own evidence. As we learn enough about different types of city and the relations between them to pick individual cities with a sharper understanding of the questions which each type may clarify, we should come back to case studies, but not case studies of the sort which have filled whole shelves of social area analysis. Armed with better general theories, and some hypotheses to take them further, we can explore cities chosen to test these ideas. Much of the evidence we shall need will be historical, dealing with the character of a community, its political leadership, public services, industrial enterprises and general culture. *Ideas for Australian Cities* by Hugh Stretton, a historically minded political scientist, comes closer to providing what we need than anything yet written in Britain.[15]

Planning and the Public

A great deal has been written about public participation in planning since the Skeffington Committee began the inquiry which led to their report on People and Planning.[16] Our own study provides no more than a postscript to that literature.

In the course of our research we have repeatedly glimpsed, though we have not paused to explore, the differing character and culture of different places and the particular aspirations and attitudes which each city tends to foster. It is no accident that nationalism and Fascism (a different movement, yet a form of English nationalism) tend to thrive not in the Conservative suburbs and shires but in the traditional strongholds of the Labour movement. It is in the old industrial areas and inner cities where working men have lost most in job opportunities, earnings and status, that hostility to 'foreigners' and to Westminster, Whitehall and the political, administrative and trade union establishments is likely to be sharpest. The timing of the revival of feminism and the cities in which the various branches of that movement tend to be strongest are easier to understand after studying our evidence about the growth of opportunities for women – particularly in white collar jobs and in the centres of service industry where these jobs are concentrated.[17] We have shown too that the educational attainment of eleven-year-olds – and probably the aspirations their parents have for them – tend to be most vigorous in places where the growth of the economy seems to encourage ambition and hope.

If the character of a city – a potentially changing character – may influence people's attitudes, then it is clear that decisions which may change a city in fundamental ways cannot be wholly validated by public preferences which themselves are the product of the environment which those very decisions may alter. Different, and potentially conflicting, preferences could be brought to bear on the decision: those held in the conditions preceding the decision, or those held under the new conditions which the decision brings about. Which, if either, should be treated as conclusive?[18]

There can be no single, authoritative answer to that question. Every change causes bereavement and grief of some kind, and sometimes that sense of loss will outweigh any gains which could be made.[19] But to advocate that planners or politicans should respond to current preferences, without considering the way in which their decisions might in time change those preferences, is deliberately to adopt a conservative bias by according greater weight to the influence of past history than to any circumstances which might in future be brought into being. Where non-marginal changes are at stake — changes sufficiently important to affect the preferences of the governed — government calls for an independent exercise of judgement: it calls for a political decision.

Planners should constantly compare their proposals with public preferences — particularly the preferences of those whom their programmes are intended to serve (the preferences of gypsies for different sites, for example — not just the preferences of the voters who all want the gypsies to go elsewhere). But the decision-maker who treats such preferences as his *only* arbiters of action is biased or naive. The capacity of planners — and politicians and public servants of all kinds — to envisage feasible and better futures not yet sanctioned by current preferences is an essential part of their professional equipment. To do that consistently and convincingly they need to know the world in which they live, and to have a vision, rooted in some understanding of the social movements and aspirations of the people whom they serve, of what that world might become.

Appendix I

Clusters

Non-Manual Group:

Family 1
   Cluster 1   London
   Cambridge
  *London

Family 2
   Cluster 2   Regional Service Centres
   Reading
  *Wallasey
  *Exeter
  *Plymouth
  *Bristol
   Cheltenham
  *Portsmouth
  *Southampton
   Tynemouth
  *Oxford
  *Bath
  *Brighton
  *York
  *Cardiff
   Aberdeen
  *Edinburgh

*The constituency boundaries and the local authority boundaries differ by less than five per cent of the population.

**These five towns were omitted from the analysis in Chapter 9. For the remaining towns in clusters 4-6 we used local authority areas for this chapter.

Family 3
Cluster 3   Resorts
Torbay
*Southend
*Bournemouth
Christchurch and Lymington
Thanet
*Blackpool
*Southport
*Hastings
Hove
Worthing

Family 4
Cluster 4   Residential Suburbs
Cheadle
**Hazelgrove
Crosby
Chertsey and Walton-on-Thames
Epsom and Ewell
Esher
Reigate
**Spelthorne
Solihull
Sutton Coldfield

Cluster 5   New Industrial Suburbs
Runcorn
Altrincham and Sale
Poole
Fareham
Watford
Gillingham
Middleton and Prestwich
Newcastle under Lyme
Halesowen and Stourbridge
Worcester
**Pudsey
Monmouth

Cluster 6   New Towns
**Wokingham
 Harlow
 Basildon
 Havant and Waterloo
 Hemel Hempstead
 Hertford and Stevenage
 Welwyn and Hatfield
 Aldridge and Brownhills
 Horsham and Crawley
**East Kilbride

Manual Group:

Family 5
Cluster 7   Welsh Mining Towns
 Aberdare
*Merthyr Tydfill
 Rhondda

Cluster 8   Engineering I
*Stockport
*Carlisle
 Chesterfield
*Derby
 Blaydon
*Darlington
 Barrow in Furness
 Eccles
*Lincoln
*Norwich
 Northampton
 Wallsend
*Ipswich
 Brighouse
 Doncaster
*Sheffield
 Wakefield
*Swansea
*Newport

Cluster 9   Textile Towns

Accrington
Ashton under Lyne
Blackburn
*Bolton
*Burnley
Bury and Radcliffe
Nelson and Colne
Oldham
Preston
*Rochdale
Rossendale
*Leicester
Bradford
Halifax
Huddersfield
Keighley

Cluster 10   Engineering II

*Luton
Eton and Slough
Bebington/and Ellesmere Port
Thurrock
*Gloucester
Gosport
Peterborough
Rochester and Chatham
Ormskirk
Stretford
*Grimsby
*Coventry
Swindon
Teesside

Cluster 11   Heavy Engineering and Coal

Chester le Street
Easington
*Hartlepool
Jarrow
Farnworth
Ince
Leigh

*St. Helens
*Wigan
 Blyth
*Dudley
*Stoke on Trent
*Walsall
*West Bromwich
*Wolverhampton
 Nuneaton
 Warley
 Barnsley
 Natley and Morley
 Dewsbury
 Pontefract and Castleford
*Rotherham

Family 6
Cluster 12   Inner Conurbations
 Birkenhead
 Gateshead
*South Shields
*Sunderland
 Bootle
*Liverpool
 Manchester
*Salford
*Warrington
 Newcastle upon Tyne
*Nottingham
*Birmingham
*Hull
*Leeds

Cluster 13   Central Scotland
*Dundee
 Coatbridge and Airdrie
 Motherwell
*Glasgow
 Greenock and Port Glasgow
 Paisley

Appendix II

The Cluster Analysis Technique

The cluster analysis algorithm used in this project was developed by Richard Webber of the Centre for Environmental Studies as part of a more general package for Liverpool City Council and Merseyside County Council (see Webber, *Liverpool Social Area Study, 1971 Data: Final Report*, PRAG TP 14 which combines initial iterative relocation with stepwise fusion). The method is as follows: the user selects up to 40 variables whose scores are standardised by the population weighted means and standard deviations of the 154 cities to be analysed. He must specify the number (q) of clusters in advance, and (q) zones are extracted and their co-ordinates are used as first approximation centroids around which the remaining zones can be grouped. The selection of the (q) starting points may be random or may be controlled by the researcher. The package then considers each of the 154 urban areas in turn, estimates its distance from each of the q starting points in n-dimensional space (where in this case n=40, the maximum number of possible classifying variables) and assigns the urban area to the closest starting point. The distance between two urban areas is estimated by calculating the difference in their standardised scores for each classifying variable, squaring the differences and summing across all 40 variables (sum of squares criterion).

When all the urban areas have been assigned to a cluster the mean of each cluster is recalculated. The original assignment is then tested to consider whether as a result of the correction of the cluster mean, any urban areas could better be assigned to another cluster. By this means the urban areas are continuously shuffled, iteration by iteration, until a stable position is reached. The distinguishing feature of this position is that no case lies closer to any other centroid than the one to which it is assigned, whilst each centroid represents the mean position of all the cases assigned to it.

From this simplified description of the cluster analysis technique it can be seen that there are three occasions on which 'subjective' judge-ments are required. These are, first, the selection of the classifying varia-bles; second, the choice of cluster starting point; and finally, deciding on the correct number of clusters. There were four basic criteria involved in these decisions:

1.   The list of variables should be comprehensive and cover as many aspects of the urban economy as possible. For this reason there was no question of using fewer than the maximum 40 variables allowed by the programme. The reason for this criterion was that the project was designed to examine distribution within all sectors of the economy.

2.   The variables should not duplicate each other.

3.   The classification produced should not only lose the smallest possible share of the original variance among classifying variables, but also lose the smallest possible share of the variance among other variables for which information was available.

4.   The classification should to a certain extent conform to the most basic understanding of the structure of urban Britain. Although this last criterion may appear more subjective than the previous ones, the first three criteria nevertheless virtually guarantee its fulfilment. It is fairly clear, for example, that a set of variables which grouped Esher and Glasgow into the same cluster would not be representative of every aspect of the urban system.

Appendix III

Variables Used in the Cluster Analysis

All variables are expressed as a number per 10,000.

1. Number of professional and managerial workers per 10,000 stated civilian heads of households (SEGs 1-4, 13).
2. Number of other non-manual workers per 10,000 stated civilian heads of households (SEGs 5, 6).
3. Number of skilled manual workers per 10,000 stated civilian heads of households (SEG 8, 9, 12, 14).
4. Number of semi-skilled manual workers per 10,000 stated civilian heads of households (SEG 7, 10, 15).
5. Number of unskilled manual workers per 10,000 stated civilian heads of households (SEG 11).
6. Number of civilian stated socio-economic groups in manufacturing and mining per 10,000 workers.
7. Number of civilian stated socio-economic groups in distribution and civilian services per 10,000 workers.
8. Number of civilian stated socio-economic groups in transport and utilities per 10,000 workers.
9. Number of civilian stated socio-economic groups self-employed per 10,000 workers.
10. Number of economically active females over 15 years old per 10,000 females over 15 years old.
11. Number of households with two or more cars per 10,000 households.
12. Number of economically active males seeking work per 10,000 economically active males.
13. Number of married women with children under 5 working more than 30 hours per 10,000 women workers.
14. Number of males sick per 10,000 economically active males.
15. Number of households in owner occupation per 10,000 households.

16.   Number of households renting from local authority or new town corporation per 10,000 households.

17.   Number of households renting privately unfurnished accommodation per 10,000 households.

18.   Number of households renting privately furnished accommodation per 10,000 households.

19.   Number of households with exclusive use of all amenities per 10,000 households.

20.   Number of households with no inside WC per 10,000 households.

21.   Number of households in shared dwellings per 10,000 households.

22.   Number of households living at a density of less than 0.5 persons per room, per 10,000 households.

23.   Number of households living at a density of more than 1.5 persons per room, per 10,000 households.

24.   Average dwelling size per 10,000 households.

25.   Number of workers with 'A' level or ONC per 10,000 workers employed.

26.   Number of workers with degree or HNC per 10,000 workers employed.

27.   Number of single women aged 15-19 economically active per 10,000 within age 15-19.

28.   Number of civilian workers travelling to work by car per 10,000 in stated civilian employment.

29.   Number of civilian workers travelling to work by bus per 10,000 in stated civilian employment.

30.   Population aged 0-4 per 10,000 population.

31.   Population aged 5-14 per 10,000 population.

32.   Population aged 15-24 per 10,000 population.

33.   Population aged 25-44 per 10,000 population.

34.   Population aged 45-64 per 10,000 population.

35.   Population aged 65+ per 10,000 population.

36.   Number of households with 2 adults and 5 children per 10,000 households.

37.   Number of single-parent households with more than 2 children per 10,000 households.

38.   Number of single non-pensioner households per 10,000 households.

39.   Number of people born in the New Commonwealth per 10,000 people.

40.   Growth in the electorate, 1955-70.

Appendix IV

Area-Based Variables for the Analysis of Educational Inputs
Described in Chapter 11

1. Total population
2. Density in persons per acre
3. Primary school population
4. Secondary school population
5. Number of primary schools maintained by the local education authority
6. Pupil teacher ratio — primary
7. Pupil teacher ratio — secondary
8. Costs of teachers' salaries per pupil — total
9. Costs of teachers' salaries per pupil — primary
10. Costs of teachers' salaries per pupil — secondary
11. Total costs per pupil
12. Total costs per pupil — primary
13. Total costs per pupil — secondary
14. Assistance to further education
15. Product of the 1p rate

(SOURCES: Institute of Municipal Treasurers and Accountants and the Scottish Education Department)

Appendix V

V Child-Based Variables for the Analysis of Social Influences on Educational Attainment

Family composition
1. Family size
2. Age of mother at birth

Grouping adopted for analysis
Numbers of children: 1, 2, 3, 4, 5+
Mothers up to and including 24; over 24.

Social status
3. Social class (father's occupation)

Initially six Registrar General's groups: I, II, III non-manual, III manual, IV, V.

4. Low incomes

Two groups: a child in the family receiving free school meals or family receiving supplementary benefit; neither of these.

5. Mother working

Four groups: full-time permanent; part-time permanent; temporary; not working or working less than one month in the past year.

6. Mother stayed on beyond minimum school leaving age.

Two groups: yes, no.

Home
7. Tenure

Two groups: owner-occupied; local authority rented, privately rented or tied to employment.

8. Crowding

Three groups: $\leqslant 1$; $\leqslant 1.5$; > 1.5 persons per room.

9. Use of hot water

Two groups: sole use; shared use or none.

10. Three amenities:
    hot water, bath, WC.

Two groups: sole use of all; absence or shared use of at least one.

School and environment

11. Public library

Four groups: goes often; goes sometimes; never goes; library not available

12. Pupil/teacher ratio

Three groups: $\leqslant 30$; $\leqslant 35$; > 35.

13. Parental contact with school

Three groups: both parents; either, neither.

14. School absences, as reported by the parent

Three groups: under 1 week; 1 week-1 month; over 1 month.

Health

15. Hospital admissions — child

Two groups: any, none.

16. Seen dentist in last year — child

Two groups: yes, no.

17. Parents' chronic illness

Three groups: either; neither; no answer.

18. Father off work through illness

Three groups: none; 1-4 weeks; 5 weeks or more.

Mobility

19. Geographical mobility

Four groups: child in same LEA from birth to 11 (i.e. same at age 0, 7, 11); same 7, 11 not 0; different at 0, 7; no data 0, 7.

20. Number of schools attended since age 5

Two groups: 1 or 2; 3 or more.

(SOURCE: National Child Development Study)

Appendix VI

Methods of Research for the Postal Survey of Chief Local Government Officers

This was the letter and questionnaire sent to Chief Education Officers to seek their help in the study. Similar letters were sent to Housing and Social Services Directors.

The jobs included in the analysis of replies to these questionnaires began with the post held in 1948, or the first post in the relevant profession if that was taken up at a later date. Posts outside local government were included, provided they fell within the official's professional field. Thus for Social Services Directors paid work in voluntary social work agencies serving a local area and university research and teaching connected with the social services were included; for Education Officers teaching and administrative posts in schools and colleges were included, and attributed to the town or county in which they stood; and for Housing Managers posts in housing associations, firms of surveyors, estate agents and landlords, and clerical and other work in relevant local government services such as Treasurer's or Surveyor's Departments were all included. (Many of the local housing authorities' functions are still performed in these departments.) The chief officer's present post was excluded (for that, by definition, would simply add one reading to every authority responding). Time spent as a student or in the armed forces, and time spent in national services without a clearly defined local territory such as Her Majesty's Inspectors of Education, the Home Office Inspectorate, or national charities such as 'War on Want' was excluded. Where a chief officer had held two or more posts with the same local authority, only one of these was counted if the others followed directly after (on the ground that to count more might only reflect the tendency of some respondents to

| **Centre for Environmental Studies** | 62 Chandos Place
London
WC2N 4HH |

Tel: 01-240 3424

From David Donnison

6 February 1976

Dear

Please may I have your help in a study of urban development and local planning policies I am making with the support of the SSRC? This part of the project has been prepared after consulting Mr. Harrison, President of the Society of Education Officers, and with the Society's encouragement.

We are trying to formulate and test some ideas about distribution of opportunities among different kinds of people in cities which develop in various ways. We are particulary interested in the fate of the poorest and most vulnerable people, but we also want to learn something about the community's leading spirits and most success-ful members, and the cities in which they spent formative stages in their careers. That is why I am writing to you and other Directors and Chief Education Officers.

I would be very grateful if you would return the short questionnaire enclosed listing the posts you have held for at least one year, noting in particular the *local authorities* for which you have worked, and the *places* where you worked during periods spent outside local government service. All personal details will of course be confidential, but I will make a general report on the findings of this study to the Society of Education Officers, which will, I hope, be communicated to you and your colleagues, if the Society thinks it would interest you.

You may know that I have recently left the Directorship of this Centre to become Chairman of the Supplementary Benefits Commis-sion, so I should explain that my SBC work leaves me one day a week to continue with research already under way at CES, and it is in this capacity that I am seeking your help.

Yours sincerely,

Please return to:

David Donnison
Centre for Enviromental Studies
62 Chandos Place
London WC2N 4HH

	YEAR APPOINTED
1. NAME	
2. PRESENT POST	
3. PREVIOUS POSTS held for one year or more, going back to the start of your professional career or to 1948 (whichever is the more recent).	
4. If one or more of these jobs had a particularly formative influence on your professional development or advancement, please note this and briefly explain why the job proved to be so important to you. (Continue overleaf if you wish).	

give more detail than others about the promotions they received within one authority's service). But if an official resigned from an authority's service, worked elsewhere for a year or more and then returned to a new post with the same authority both jobs were included.

Local government in England was completely reorganised on 1 April 1974, less than two years before these questionnaires went out. This presented a problem because many authorities then changed in size, population and name. Devonshire, for example, might be mentioned more often than Exeter because the two authorities were combined for education and social service purposes at that point under the name of Devonshire. Posts taken up after reorganisation were therefore excluded. As the respondents' current posts, which were in any case excluded, had nearly all begun with reorganisation, this lost virtually no data.

London presented more difficult problems because local government in the capital was reorganised in 1965. Southwark, for example, may appear more often than Bermondsey simply because the two authorities were then amalgamated under the name of Southwark, and the GLC was an altogether different entity from the LCC, with a much larger area but much fewer powers. These complications compelled us to exclude London from the main analysis and treat it separately, later in the chapter.

A theoretical probability that any particular authority would be mentioned had then to be estimated in order to compare that with the actual number of mentions each received. The simplest assumption to make was a random one: an authority's need for a service and the number of posts it would offer would be proportional to its population. That assumption would suit a service such as education better than most, because everyone needs education at some stage of their lives, and the great majority attend schools maintained by their local education authority. Even in education, however, the proportion of the population undergoing education may vary a great deal from place to place. The demands on a housing service will vary much more, in ways not directly related to the numbers of people in the area.

Population offered a simple criterion: but population at what date? We took the median date at which the careers of each of these groups of officials began. The mid-points of the periods which had elapsed since then occurred in the early 1960s, soon after the 1961 Census.

Thus the Registrar General's estimates of the home populations of these authorities at 30 June 1961 were taken as the basis for the analysis. For each authority that was expressed as a proportion of the population of Great Britain at the same date. (Because some officials had worked in Wales and Scotland this seemed marginally more appropriate than a comparison with the population of England.) For each of the three professions in turn the number of times each authority was mentioned was compared with the total number of mentions received by all authorities. Finally the two ratios were compared with each other, thus:

$$\frac{\text{Number of times authority } A \text{ mentioned}}{\text{Total mentions of all authorities}} \div \frac{\text{Population of authority } A}{\text{Total population of Great Britain}}$$

If for a particular authority the two ratios were the same, it would receive a score of 1.00, which meant that it had been mentioned as often as its population would have led us to expect. Likewise, an authority scoring 3.00 was mentioned three times as often as its population alone would have led us to expect.

References and Notes

Preface
1. D. Donnison, 'What is the "Good City"?', *New Society*, 15 December 1973.

1. Town Planning in Britain: the Coalition of 1947
1. For example W. Ashworth, *The Genesis of Modern British Town Planning*, Routledge & Kegan Paul, 1954; L. Mumford, *The City in History; its Origins, its Transformations and its Prospects*, Secker and Warburg, 1961; C. and R. Bell *City Fathers; the Early History of Town Planning in Britain*, Penguin, 1972; and M. Clawson and P. Hall, *Planning and Urban Growth. An Anglo-American Comparison*, John Hopkins University Press, 1973.
2. David Eversley, *The Planner in Society. The Changing Role of a Profession*, Faber, 1973, has told both parts of the story — without detachment.
3. Official Report, 1946-47, Vol. 432; Second Reading, Town and Country Planning Bill, 29 January 1947, Col. 947 *et seq.*
4. *Report of the Royal Commission on the Distribution of the Industrial Population*, (The Barlow Report), Cmd. 6153, HMSO, 1940.
5. Patrick Abercrombie, *Greater London Plan 1944*, HMSO, 1945.
6. Official Report, 1945-46, Vol. 422; Second Reading of New Towns Bill, 8 May 1946; Col. 1088 *et seq.*
7. Mr. Molson, Col. 1108.
8. *Report of the Commission on the Third London Airport*, Note of Dissent by Colin Buchanan, HMSO, 1971, p. 149.
9. See J. B. McLoughlin, *Control and Urban Planning*, Faber, 1973, p. 155.
10. This point is vividly made by an Australian, Hugh Stretton, in *Housing and Government*, 1974 Boyer Lectures, Australian Broadcasting Commission, 1974.

11. J. B. Cullingworth, *Environmental Planning. Vol. I. Reconstruction and Land Use Planning, 1939-1947*, HMSO, 1975, p. 149.

12. *Final Report of the Expert Committee on Compensation and Betterment* (Uthwatt Report), Cmd. 6386, 1942.

13. Official Report, Vol. 432, Col. 963.

14. F. S. W. Craig, *British General Election Manifestos, 1918-1966*, Political Reference Publications, 1970.

15. These trends and their implications for urban planning and politics have been well described by Marion Clawson and Peter Hall, *Planning and Urban Growth. An Anglo-American Comparison*, John Hopkins University Press, 1973, and Oliver P. Williams, *Metropolitan Political Analysis. A Social Approach*, Free Press, and Collier-Macmillan, 1971.

2. The Coalition Breaks Up

1. *Housing Statistics* and *Housing and Construction Statistics*, HMSO, quarterly.

2. For an account of this boom, see Oliver Mariott, *The Property Boom*, Hamish Hamilton, 1967.

3. British examples include: Norman Dennis, *Public Participation and Planners' Blight*, Faber, 1972; R. Bailey, *The Squatters*, Penguin, 1973; Cynthia Cockburn, *The Local State*, Pluto Press, 1977; David Donnison, 'Micropolitics of the City' in Donnison and David Eversley (eds.), *London: Urban Patterns, Problems and Policies*, Heinemann Educational Books, 1973; J. Ferris, *Participation in Urban Planning: the Barnsbury Case*, Occasional Papers in Social Administration, Bell, 1972; Jan O'Malley, *The Politics of Community Action*, Spokesman, 1977.

4. *Housing Statistics*.

5. *Planning and the Future*, by a working party of the Royal Town Planning Institute, the Institution of Civil Engineers, and the Royal Institution of Chartered Surveyors, RTPI, 1976, p. 102.

6. *The South East Study, 1961-1981*, HMSO, 1964.

7. Planning Advisory Group, *The Future of Development Plans*, HMSO, 1965.

8. *Report of the Committee on Housing in Greater London* (Milner Holland Report), Cmnd. 2605, HMSO, 1965.

9. *Report on Higher Education 1961-63* (Robbins Report), HMSO, 1963; and *Children and their Primary Schools: a Report of the Central Advisory Council for Education (England)* (Plowden Report), HMSO, 1967.

208 The Good City

10. *Report of the Committee on Local Authority and Allied Personal Social Services* (Seebohm Report), Cmnd. 3703, HMSO, 1968.
11. This change is traced by Simon Jenkins, *Landlords to London*, Constable, 1975.
12. *People and Planning*, HMSO, 1969.
13. Evelyn Sharp shows how important was the planners' contribution to this debate: *The Ministry of Housing and Local Government*, Allen and Unwin, 1969, p. 139. Cynthia Cockburn traces the links between new thinking about local government and planning in *The Local State*, Pluto Press, 1977, Chapter 1.
14. T. A. Broadbent, *Planning and Profit in the Urban Economy*, Methuen, 1977, p. 218.
15. The movement can be dated by some of the most widely quoted books it generated: John Friend and Neil F. Jessop, *Local Government and Strategic Choice*, Tavistock, 1969; J. Brian McLoughlin, *Urban and Regional Planning: a Systems Approach*, Faber, 1969; George F. Chadwick, *A Systems View of Planning*, Pergamon, 1971; and J. D. Stewart, *Management in Local Government: a Viewpoint*, Charles Knight, 1973.
16. For example, Department of the Environment, *New Local Authorities, Management and Structure* (Bains Report), HMSO, 1972.
17. T. A. Broadbent, himself highly qualified in his field, gives a critical account of the way in which new analytical techniques were introduced into planning and transport studies without an understanding of their intellectual foundations or political implications in *Planning and Profit in the Urban Economy*, Chapter 6.
18. *The Plan for Milton Keynes*, Milton Keynes Development Corporation, 1970, Vol. 1, para. 26.
19. F. J. C. Amos, *Social Malaise in Liverpool: Interim Report on Social Problems and their Distribution*, Liverpool Corporation, 1970.
20. Department of the Environment, *Greater London Development Plan: Report of the Panel of Enquiry*, 1973, Vol. 1, pp. 24-7.
21. London Docklands Study Team, *Docklands: Redevelopment Proposals for East London*, R. Travers Morgan and Partners, 1973; pp. 19-20.
22. Joint Circular on Structure Plans, Department of the Environment 98/74, Welsh Office 168/74, 10 July 1974.
23. Madeline Drake, Brian McLoughlin, Robin Thompson and Jennifer Thornley, *Aspects of Structure Planning in Britain*, CES RP20,

Centre for Environmental Studies, 1975.

24. Department of the Environment and Welsh Offices, *Development Control Statistics*, 1975/76.

25. John Burrows, 'Vacant Urban Land — a Continuing Crisis', *The Planner*, Vol. 64, No. 1, January 1978.

26. *Planning and the Future*, pp. 76-7 RTPI, 1976.

27. This summary was provided by the Working Group's Chairman in response to a review of their Report. Sylvia Law, 'Planning and the Future. A Commentary on the Debate', *Town Planning Review*, Vol. 48, No. 4, October 1977. See also 'Planning and the Future. A Review Symposium', *Town Planning Review*, Vol. 48, No. 3, July 1977; and Tony Eddison, 'Planning and the Future. A Professional Response', *The Planner*, Vol. 63, No. 2, March 1977.

28. *Policy for the Inner Cities*, Cmnd. 6845, HMSO, 1977.

3. Social Policy Goes Spatial

1. Many of the developments traced in this chapter are explored at greater length and interpreted in different ways by Cynthia Cockburn in *The Local State*, Pluto Press, 1977. For a briefer discussion see David Donnison, 'Policies for Priority Areas', *Journal of Social Policy*, Vol. 3, No. 2, 1974, reprinted by the Centre for Environmental Studies as CES Reprint No. 20.

2. *Family and Kinship in East London*, Routledge and Kegan Paul, 1957, p. 166.

3. See, for example, Bleddyn Davies, *Social Needs and Resources in Local Services*, Michael Joseph, 1968.

4. *Children and Their Primary Schools*, Report of the Central Advisory Council for Education (England), HMSO, 1967.

5. *Report of the Committee on Local Authority and Allied Personal Social Services*, Cmnd. 3703, HMSO, 1968.

6. *Housing in Greater London*, Cmnd. 2605, HMSO, 1965.

7. Home Office, Urban Programme Circular No. 1, October 1968.

8. Calouste Gulbenkian Foundation, *Working with Communities*, National Council of Social Service, 1963; *Community Work and Social Change*, Longman, 1968; and *Current Issues in Community Work*, Routledge and Kegan Paul, 1973.

9. These questions were revealingly discussed by Richard White in 'Lawyers and the Enforcement of Rights', in Pauline Morris, Richard White and Philip Lewis, *Social Needs and Legal Action*, Martin Robertson, 1973.

10. Brian Abel-Smith and Peter Townsend, *The Poor and the Poorest*,

Bell, 1965, was a forerunner of many other studies.

11. Summarised by Ronald Davie, Neville Butler and Harvey Goldstein in *From Birth to Seven*, Longman, 1972. See also David Donnison (ed.), *A Pattern of Disadvantage*, National Foundation for Educational Research, 1972.

12. I. S. Holtermann, *Census Indicators of Urban Deprivation* Working Note No. 6, Department of the Environment, 1975, p. 10.

13. *Policy for the Inner Cities*, Cmnd. 6845, HMSO, June 1977, para. 71. For an account of most of these projects see *Gilding the Ghetto. The State and the Poverty Experiements*, CDP Inter-Project Editorial Team, Home Office (Urban Deprivation Unit), 1977.

14. Community Development Project Information and Intelligence Unit, *The Inter-Project Report*, 1974, and *Forward Plan 1975-76*, 1975.

15. *Forward Plan 1975-76*, p. 2.

16. *Forward Plan 1975-76*; pp. 1, 6 and 16.

17. Royal Commission on the Distribution of Income and Wealth, Report No. 5, Third Report on the Standing Reference, Cmnd. 6999, 1977; and Background Paper No. 4, *The Distribution of Income in Eight Countries*, HMSO, 1977.

18. Alan Murie, Pat Niner and Christopher Watson, *Housing Policy and the Housing System*, Allen and Unwin, 1976, Chapter 7.

19. *The Politics of Community Action*, Spokesman Books, 1977.

20. C. G. Pickvance (Ed.), *Urban Sociology: Critical Essays*, Tavistock, 1976, p. 178.

21. C. Cockburn, *The Local State*, Pluto Press, 1977.

22. Charles Booth, *Life and Labour of the People*, Macmillan, 1892, vol. I, p. 154.

23. Hugh Stretton, *Urban Planning in Rich and Poor Countries*, Oxford University Press, 1978; Chapters 10 and 12.

24. Coventry CDP, *Coventry and Hillfields: Prosperity and the Persistence of Inequality*, 1975, p. 40 *et seq.*

4. Questions and Hypotheses

1. *The Disadvantages of Inequality*, MacDonald and Janes for P.E.P., 1976, pp. 128, 178 and 192.

2. For a perceptive discussion of these and other questions explored in this chapter, see Wilbur R. Thompson, 'Internal and External Factors in the Development of Urban Economies', in H. S. Perloff and L. Wingo, *Issues in Urban Economics*, John Hopkins Press, 1968.

3. The same point is made for American society by Andrew M. Greeley in 'American Catholics — Making it or Losing it?', *The Public Interest*, No. 28, Summer 1972, and some of its implications are explored by Anthony H. Pascal in 'Black Gold and Black Capitalism', *The Public Interest*, No. 19, Spring 1970.
4. Peter Willmott traces such a process in *The Evolution of a Community*, Routledge and Kegan Paul, 1963.

5. National Trends in the Labour Market

1. Central Statistical Office, *Social Trends, 9* , HMSO, 1978; Table 1.12, p. 38.
2. R. Bacon and W. Eltis, *Britain's Economic Problem: Too Few Producers*, Macmillan, 1976.
3. *Economic Progress Report*, HM Treasury, February 1976.
4. B. Fine and L. Harris, 'The British Economy since March 1974', *Bulletin of Conference of Socialist Economists*, 1975.
5. Estimates by Peter Riddell, *Financial Times*, 4 April 1978.
6. Censuses of Population.
7. Calculated from the Census of Employment.
8. W. B. Reddaway, *The Effects of the Selective Employment Tax: First Report on the Distributive Trades*, HMSO, 1970.
9. Both figures calculated from the Census of Employment.
10. *Education, Industry and People*, 1977, Josiah Mason Memorial Lecture, University of Birmingham, 1978.
11. H. Braverman, *Labor and Monopoly Capital*, Monthly Review Press, 1974.

6. Urban Patterns

1. Marion Clawson and Peter Hall, *Planning and Urban Growth*, 1973.
2. Richard Webber, *Liverpool Social Area Study, 1971 Data: Final Report*, Prag Technical Papers, PRAG TP 14, December 1975, reprinted April 1976, Centre for Environmental Studies, London.
3. These indicators roughly correspond to those used in three other studies: (i) John Edwards, *The Identification of Areas of Deprivation: Urban Programme Research*, Home Officer, (ii) North West Interprofessional Group, *Local Authority Needs and Resources: the effect of the rate support grant in the North West*, CES RP12, 1975; and (iii) I. S. Holtermann, *Census Indicators of Urban Deprivation. Great Britain*, Working Note No. 6, Department of the Environment, 1975.

4. For example see C. A. Moser and Wolf Scott, *British Towns*, Oliver and Boyd, 1961.

5. Alan Evans, *Economics of Residential Location*, Macmillan, 1973.

7. Different Kinds of Towns

1. Department of Education and Science, *Statistics of Education*, Vol. 2, HMSO, Annual.

8. From Towns to People

1. See the last five variables in Appendix III.

2. The ranges of scores shown in columns (c) and (f) of this table could be standardised by showing the ratio of these scores to the mean of the highest and lowest scores, but since the results of this more complex formula would be the same (as the reader can verify for himself) the simpler presentation seemed preferable.

9. Inner City Unemployment

1. Walter Oi, 'Labour as a Quasi Fixed Factor', *Journal of Political Economy*, 1962.

2. Melvin Reder, 'The Theory of Occupational Wage Differentials', *American Economic Review*, 1955.

3. J. T. Corkindale, Employment in the Conurbations, Inner City Employment Conference, York, 1976.

4. Department of Employment.

5. Op. cit.

6. The Costs of Industrial Change, CDP, 1977.

7. N. Bosanquet and P. B. Doeringer, 'Is There a Dual Labour Market in Great Britain?', *Economic Journal*, June 1973.

8. The towns in each cluster are listed in Appendix II.

9. Cities in Decline, 1976.

10. See Table 5.4

11. D. B. Massey & R. A. Meegan, *The Geography of Industrial Reorganisation: the spacial effects of the restructuring of the electrical engineering corporation*. Progress in Planning, Vol. 10, Part 3, Pergamon, 1979.

12. *Canning Town to North Woolwich. The Aims of Industry?*, Canning Town CDP, 1977.

13. *Inner City Partnership Programme 1979-1982*, Birmingham Inner City Partnership, 1978.

10. Middle England

1. Michael Harloe, *Swindon: A Town in Transition*, Heinemann, 1975, p. 84.
2. P. H. Levin, *Government and the Planning Process*, Allen and Unwin, 1976: K. Hudson, *An Awkward Size for a Town*, David and Charles, 1967; and Harloe, op. cit.
3. John Betjeman in *Continual Dew*, John Murray, 1937 (reprinted 1977).

11. Education: Cause or Effect?

1. The main publications reporting on this study are R. Davie, N. Butler and H. Goldstein, *From Birth to Seven*, Longman, 1972; P. Wedge and H. Prosser, *Born to Fail?*, Arrow Books, 1973; and K. Fogelman (ed.), *Britain's Sixteen Year Olds*, National Children's Bureau, 1976.
2. H. Robinson, P. Gorbach and P. Wedge, *Urban and Regional Differences in Children's Educational Attainment*, National Children's Bureau, Report to sponsors, 1977.
3. Northern Region Strategy Team, *The Characteristics of the Unemployed in the Northern Region, 1966-1974*, Technical Report No. 6, 1975, p. 42.
4. For a review of research on the effects of teachers' expectations on the attainments of their pupils, see Doria Pilling and Mia Kellmer Pringle, *Controversial Issues in Child Development*, Paul Elek, 1978, Part IV.
5. Eric Midwinter, 'The Key to those LEA League Tables', *Where?*, no. 77, February 1973, p. 53.
6. For a summary of the evidence about school leaving ages in the economically developed countries, see *Second Report of the Public Schools Commission*, Vol. I, pp. 21-4, HMSO, 1970.

12. Paths to Glory

1. P. R. Gould and R. R. White, 'The Mental Maps of British School Leavers', *Regional Studies*, Vol. 2, No. 2, 1968, p. 161.

13. Conclusions

1. See Chapters 5 and 9 for the evidence on which most of this section is based.
2. Chapters 6, 7 and 8 present most of the evidence summarised in this section.
3. The one point on which our data cannot be reconciled with these

generalisations deal with educational attainment in Glasgow and
Dundee. See page 150 for a discussion of this problem.

4. H. Kasper, 'Measuring the Labour Market Costs of Housing Dislo-
cation', *Urban Studies Working Paper No. 4*, University of Glasgow,
1971.

5. R. Minns and J. Thornley, *State Shareholding: The Role of Local
and Regional Authorities*, Macmillan, 1978.

6. Cmnd. 6845, HMSO, 1977.

7. Michael Liffman, *Power to the Poor*, Allen and Unwin, 1978.

8. P. Sadler, B. Archer and C. Owen, *Regional Income Multipliers*,
Bangor Occasional Papers in Economics. No. 1, University of
Wales Press, 1973.

9. R. Kirwan and D. B. Martin, *The Economics of Urban Residential
Renewal and Improvement*, Centre for Environmental Studies
Working Paper, 77, 1972.

10. Kasper, op. cit.

11. See O. Marriott, *The Property Boom*, Hamish Hamilton, 1967,
for some of the more dramatic examples of 'planning bargains'
of this sort. For a fuller and more recent discussion of the issue
see Gwyneth Kirk, *Sociology of Land Use Planning: Southwark's
Redevelopment Plans*, Ph.D. Thesis, University of London, 1978.

12. Madeline Drake, Brian McLoughlin, Robin Thompson and Jennifer
Thornley, *Aspects of Structure Planning in Britain*, CES RP20,
Centre for Environmental Studies, 1975, pp. 203 *et seq.*

13. See A. J. Fielding, *Internal Migration in England and Wales*, Centre
for Environmental Studies, University Working Paper 14, 1972.

14. For an analysis of these issues in one sector of the urban economy,
see M. Harloe, R. Issacharoff and R. Minns, *The Organization of
Housing*, Heinemann Educational Books, 1974.

15. Georgian House, Melbourne, 1971.

16. *People and Planning*, HMSO, 1969.

17. David Donnison, 'Feminism's Second Wave and Supplementary
Benefit', *The Political Quarterly*, Vol. 49, No. 3, July-September
1978.

18. This is the index number problem in a new guise. Should changes
in the cost of living taking place over a period of time be measured
by comparing the prices of a basket of goods bought at the start of
the period or the prices of a different basket bought at the end of
the period — the differences being due partly to the price changes
themselves?

19. See Peter Marris, *Loss and Change*, Routledge and Kegan Paul,
1974, for a thoughtful discussion of these issues.

Index

Tables, figures and maps are not indexed here. They are listed on page ix.

Names of towns included in the cluster analysis are indexed under 'Towns'. Types of towns adopted for this analysis are indexed under 'Clusters'. Other place names are listed under their names.